Awaken the Leader in You

Praise for the book

Mitesh has written a wonderful book, especially his chapter on Emotional Intelligence has very effectively cited examples of how, emotions if directed and managed well, can lead to a superior and fulfilled life. In a high demanding corporate environment of today absence of emotional intelligence can lead to situations of personality clash, in turn impacting organization effectiveness at large. In a highly technology intensive environment, emotional intelligence will lead to creating the right balance.

According to one school of thought, individuals are born emotionally intelligent and cannot be developed. However, in this chapter Mitesh has shared smart tips on how one can actually develop emotional intelligence.

The beauty of Mitesh Khatri's approach to the topic lies in its simplicity. He has used relevant examples of renowned personalities, as well as his personal experiences that readers will find easy to relate to. Mitesh has created opportunities for readers to actively engage themselves through exercises on emotional intelligence.

Amitrajit Ghosh, Deputy General Manager HR,
Dow Chemical International Pvt Limited

Mitesh in his very simple yet livid manner has put forth a beautiful concept of Trust Bank Account (TBA). The concept is so powerfully delivered by him that it gets permanently registered in your mind as soon as you read it.

Consciously or unconsciously one immediately starts practicing the TBA method. It's like opening an instant bank account, as you start making your cash and cheque deposits right away. You instantly get into the habit of creating your trust bank account with people and start making rich deposits in to them.

Himanshu Vyapak, Deputy CEO,
Reliance Capital Asset Management Limited

Mitesh's conclusion that values are what you give high or low priority is so simple but still so profound statement. Every parent wishes to imbibe good values in their children. As it is believed, that values are the foundation on which the character and personality of an individual is built. We enroll them in the good schools in the pursuit of giving them the best value based education, live in good locality to ensure their children have good surrounding, give lectures on good behaviour and bad behaviour and how it would influence their values.

As Mitesh writes our highest desires may not necessarily be our highest values. He has beautifully defined the word power and linked it with values in his chapter.

Viju Gangadharan, Competency Development & Training Manager,
Tieto Software Technologies Pvt. Ltd.

Indeed an exhilarating experience – full of energy, enthusiasm, motivation and message galore…that's how I would describe Mitesh. Hats off to your energy and your ability to transmit energy. Keep spreading energy, keep communicating messages all in your inimitable style.....God bless!!

Mr Yugal Sikri, Head of Global Marketing,
Ranbaxy Laboratories Ltd.

The first point that Mitesh mentioned in his chapter on *Charismatic Leadership* is "Think before you commit". This is an important *strategy* that I follow. Because with every announced commitment what you do is -increase expectation. Once you increase expectation and then do not deliver, it creates trust deficit. When there is a trust deficit, the very essence of leadership is lost. So it is important that we *Think* before we commit. Thinking means analysis, thinking means self-talk, where we evaluate the possibility of success and we plan for success.

Another point that is really interesting – "Apologize for your mistakes without giving excuses". Let me tell you – it is very difficult to say "I am sorry", especially to your team members. It is something that has always helped me. Saying sorry for mistakes creates a culture of performance and creates a culture of accountability. It creates trust, it helps in aligning the team together and therefore it helps in getting results.

Suva Chattopadhyay, General Manager – Sales & Marketing,
Abbott Truecare Pharma Pvt. Ltd.

AWAKEN

THE

LEADER

IN

YOU

Mitesh Khatri & Indu Khatri

JAICO PUBLISHING HOUSE

Ahmedabad Bangalore Bhopal Bhubaneswar Chennai
Delhi Hyderabad Kolkata Lucknow Mumbai

Published by Jaico Publishing House
A-2 Jash Chambers, 7-A Sir Phirozshah Mehta Road
Fort, Mumbai - 400 001
jaicopub@jaicobooks.com
www.jaicobooks.com

© Mitesh Khatri & Indu Khatri

AWAKEN THE LEADER IN YOU
ISBN 978-81-8495-383-1

First Jaico Impression: 2013
Ninth Jaico Impression: 2015

Printed by
Repro India Limited
Plot No. 50/2, T.T.C. MIDC Industrial Area
Mahape, Navi Mumbai - 400 710

Dedicated to all my readers, who are committed to learn and practice Leadership skills, and make this world a better place to live by becoming better human beings.

Firewalking session with Mitesh Khatri

Contents

Foreword

I f you were asked to pick the one thing that would enable you to sprint across a path strewn with jagged pieces of glass and then across a carpet of burning coals, you would most likely choose a pair of tough thermal shoes.

Few if any would choose a motivational speaker!

Yet on that very wet afternoon in the salubrious surroundings of Lavasa, when my team and I walked barefoot, first on pieces of glass and then on burning coals, we had nothing to protect our soles except the belief instilled in us by Mitesh Khatri that we could do it! And we did it… not just a few of us, but every member of the team

Fortunately, it is not often in life that we have to walk over broken glass or burning charcoal; but the journey of a leader is not less arduous.

Awaken the Leader in You is that practical guide for anyone who undertakes this arduous journey of a leader.

Most readers of this book would have already discovered their own set of practices that contribute to making them successful leaders. As part of my own experiments with leadership concepts, I had defined my role only as "creating an environment where entrepreneurial managers will not only be recognized but will be rewarded as well". Mitesh's book introduced me to this powerful concept of "entrepreneurial mindset". This approach helped me create a high performance and sustainable team of managers who not only delivered on their organizational objectives but also rewarded me with the highest "employee engagement" scores in my organization.

An organization where the culture fosters an "entrepreneurial mindset" in its managers cannot but be a successful organization.

Perhaps the most endearing feature of this book is the number of incisive behavioral checklists designed to provide a reality check on your current state of mind. My advice to you is, be honest to yourself when you answer them!

Subbarao Gudipaty, Senior Vice President, Leading Multinational Bank

Why Read This Book?

There are many books on leadership skills; then why have I written another book on this topic and why should you read it? Because this book is based on my leadership workshops, which have been highly successful, results-oriented and have had long-lasting impact on many organizations. The tools and techniques I use are extremely simple to understand and implement. But more specifically, I feel you should read this book because it has the following features:

1. A new approach to leadership, which is required in the 21st century.
2. Exercises and Techniques to make sure that you are able to achieve specific results from every chapter.
3. To the point and simple, to ensure you find it is easy to understand and enjoy every chapter without any complicated jargon.
4. Covers multiple aspects of leadership, which have been validated by some of the best leaders of our country.
5. Access Videos to the Leadership stories used in the book
6. Download Exercises, Techniques from my website for further use
7. Access Video Tutorial on each chapter from www.miteshkhatri/BookResources
8. Connect with me on Facebook for personal interaction

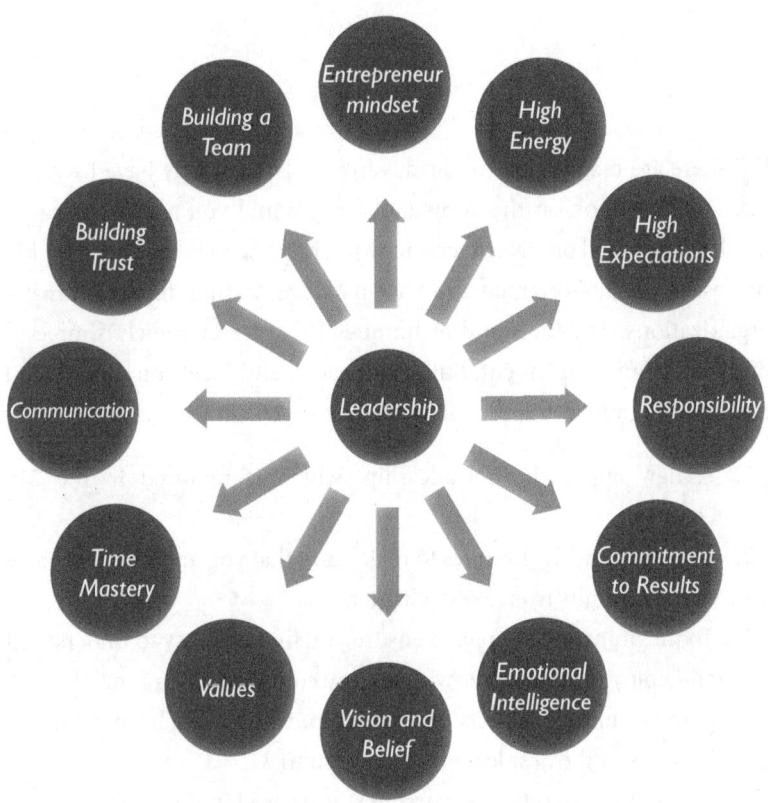

The Various Aspects of Leadership

1

The Employee Mindset vs the Entrepreneur Mindset

Hello Reader! You and I have something in common here. We are both interested in learning about leadership and growing as leaders. So before you read on, I want to congratulate you because you are one of the few people in the world who is willing to walk the path of leadership. And while it is a challenging journey, one that requires patience and perseverance, I can promise it will be worth the effort.

I have been training the corporate world for more than ten years now, and I have had the privilege to work with more than 50,000 executives across the country, in more than 80 multinational organizations. During this journey, I have always found two kinds of people in all organizations. The first category comprises those I would call Ordinary People who:

▶ Don't take ownership for their work.
▶ Don't work seriously.
▶ Make excuses and break commitments.
▶ Focus only on their personal goals, not on the organizational goals.
▶ Have poor communication skills.

▶ Don't manage their time well.
▶ Hardly upgrade their skills.
▶ Don't get along with their peers, line managers and subordinates.
▶ Keep complaining and blaming others and thus
▶ Perform ordinarily and grow slowly within their organizations.

The amazing part is that in these same organizations, I also meet the second category of people – the Extraordinary Leaders who:

▶ Always take ownership for their work.
▶ Take their work seriously.
▶ Never make excuses and keep to their commitments regularly.
▶ Focus on their organizational goals, not only on personal goals.
▶ Have excellent communication skills.
▶ Manage their time very efficiently.
▶ Keep upgrading their skills.
▶ Find new ways to get along with their peers, line managers and subordinates.
▶ Create solutions, take responsibility and thus
▶ Perform extraordinarily well and grow fast within their organizations.

When I see ordinary people and extraordinary leaders working together in the same organizations, I cannot help but ask myself:

• Why is it that some people are ordinary, while others are extraordinary?
• Do some people have less potential, making them ordinary and stalling their growth?
• Are some people born with extra potential, allowing them to grow fast and be extraordinary leaders?

My more than ten years of behavioral study immediately tells me 'No!' There is no difference in the inherent potential and abilities of people.

We are born with the same infinite potential. And I believe that within every ordinary person, there lies an extraordinary leader. And that is the intention of this book – to *Awaken The Leader In You.*

So, if all of us have the same infinite potential, then what is the difference between ordinary people and extraordinary leaders?

With years of research and understanding, I found an answer that was so simple, it blew my mind. The answer was also a very practical one: something I realized I could use to help anybody transform from an ordinary performer to an extraordinary one. I began sharing this discovery in my leadership workshops and helping people become leaders by choice. Because once you knew the exact difference between ordinary people and extraordinary leaders, then you could awaken the leader within as well! This is exactly what happened with all my participants.

The feedback from my workshops was great. I began receiving emails from CEOs, COOs, Directors, HR Heads and others, all sharing with me stories of how their staff had achieved extraordinary targets; how they had become more focused towards their organizational goals; and especially how they had started performing like extraordinary leaders. The best part was that these results were created by people who were ordinary performers before they attended my workshop. It felt like I had discovered some kind of magic that transformed ordinary people into extraordinary leaders. This was a great breakthrough for both my clients and me. I have thus decided to share this discovery with as many people as I can, and help them through this book to become leaders and create extraordinary results in their lives.

The difference between ordinary people and extraordinary leaders is actually very simple, and yet it is so profound it can open up the flood gates of high performance in any ordinary employee who wants to become an extraordinary leader. It is *this* difference that I am going to explore and help you understand.

Let me give you an example here. Many people play cricket, but not everyone is Sachin Tendulkar. There is a difference between how an ordinary person bats and how Sachin bats. Now, what if you knew the art of how Sachin bats; how he thinks in pressure situations and makes so many world records? When you understand this difference, you too can transform from an ordinary batsman to a master of the craft like Sachin Tendulkar.

Would you agree that it's easier to excel by learning from other people's successes, instead of re-inventing the wheel through your own personal experiences? If you truly want to become a leader, the fastest way is to understand *what* leaders do *differently*. So starting now in the following pages, I am going to reveal to you what I have discovered with many years of research: the basic difference between ordinary people and leaders **is their mindset**.

Yes, it is simply their mindset that differentiates them. Now I hear you say, 'What is so great about that? I already knew that!' Well, there's more; because there is a specific type of mindset difference that I am talking about, which is:

Ordinary people have the Employee Mindset while leaders have the Entrepreneur Mindset.

Yes. This is the basic difference.

- Ordinary people work with the Employee mindset, i.e., they believe they are *just* doing a *job*
- Extraordinary leaders work with the Entrepreneur mindset, i.e., they believe they *own* their organization

Let me explain this in some detail. The mindset that governs ordinary people is that of the employee; that is, they work in an organization thinking that it is *just* a *job* and nothing more. They lack a sense of ownership and pride in their work. It is because of this, that when an organization goes through its dark days (as every organization does at some point), the employee mindset are the first to quit and run. This is because it is easy for them to leave something that they never felt any ownership towards in the first place.

On the other hand, leaders work with the entrepreneur mindset. This means, they always work in an organization thinking it is their own organization. So even when things become really difficult, these are the people who stand by their organization and prove their loyalty by giving their best, even though they cannot receive the best from their organization at that point in time.

Think about it! If you really owned a business and the market was down, would you stand by your business and give it your best even though you may not receive the best returns at that time? I am sure you would. Any *real* business owner would!

But there can be some misunderstanding with the terms 'employee mindset' and 'entrepreneur mindset'. Let's get rid of that before we proceed. Here are some common questions related to the idea of these mindsets:

- Is it necessary for a person to have his own business to demonstrate the entrepreneur mindset and work like a leader?
- Is it a fact that professionals doing a job will always have the employee mindset and never an entrepreneur one?

The answer to both these questions is that leadership is simply a way of thinking, as the word 'mindset' suggests. However, these two mindsets are not exclusive to salaried professionals or business owners. These terms are used to suggest the kinds of attitudes and relationships people have with their work. Hence, I believe a person doing a job can demonstrate the entrepreneur mindset and work as if he owns the organization. At the same time, a person who owns his business can also have the employee mindset and not take any ownership of it.

Have you met people in organizations who are salaried employees, but work like entrepreneurs? Have you met people who behave as if they *own* their projects, their teams, their organizations? These are the people who eventually become leaders in any organization, because of their entrepreneurial mindsets. Designation and authority are things that come to them sooner or later because of their entrepreneurial mindset. Here is an example of such an employee who had all the important characteristics of a leader.

This young man was an employee of the Indian Railways as a Train Ticket Examiner (TTE) from 2001 to 2003. Now, most employees at this position may not have a great future ahead, but I believe that the future of a person depends on his own mindset. If an employee demonstrates the entrepreneur mindset, sooner or later he will definitely get the right opportunities. And when they do get the right opportunities, the leader within them will make the best of them.

This is exactly what this young man did. He continued being a leader and did his job with 100% ownership wherever he worked. As a result, opportunities kept coming to him and he kept growing. This young man is an idol and inspiration for most Indians today, his name is M S Dhoni – captain of Indian cricket team.

Some people might say that Dhoni was born talented and was destined to be a legend of the Indian cricket team, but this is just an excuse made by employee mindset people, to not understand what it takes to practice true leadership.

The point is that an employee also can have the entrepreneur mindset and act like a leader. This is because leadership has nothing to do with being in a job or a certain position, or owning a business; it's all about the mindset!

I am sure you have also met businessmen who behave rudely with their customers, almost as if it is not their own business that they are running. They behave poorly with their employees, almost as if they don't care to get along with them. These are people who may own businesses, but possess the employee mindset, i.e. they work as if they are just doing a job. Here is an example:

A typical example of how businessmen behave when they have the employee mindset is seen in many local shopping areas of Indian cities, where there are small shops which have been running for many years without much growth.

For instance, if you ever come to Pune in Maharashtra, there is a famous local shopping area at Laxmi Road. In this area, it is very common to find many shop-owners talking rudely to their customers, not taking ownership for what they sell, and frequently getting into arguments with their customers. If you buy something from Laxmi Road and reach home to find that the product is defective, chances are you will never get a refund or exchange on the item. The shopkeeper would take no ownership for the product once it has left his shop. This happens because even though they own businesses of their own, some of them still have the employee mindset which stops them from making their businesses grow, because they lack the long-term vision that an entrepreneur has. They function with the limited perspective of the employee, who has to get through the day and earn some money through the work he does.

But in the same market, you will find people who have the entrepreneur mindset and their businesses grow within no time. For example, in the same area – Laxmi Road, there is a shop called Jaihind Stores which started off as a very small venture many years ago.

Today it has four huge branches in Pune – all of them doing extraordinary business. It has in fact become a market leader in the city. This is because of the entrepreneur mindset of the owners. There are other shops on Laxmi Road which started around the same time as Jaihind Stores, but they haven't met with the kind of success that Jaihind has. So you see, having a business does not qualify anyone to be a leader, because leadership is about having the entrepreneur mindset, and anyone can develop this mindset irrespective of whether one is a salaried professional or a business-owner.

In organizations where I conduct training sessions, I see many people functioning with the employee mindset. And that is the reason that they don't grow. They have very little work satisfaction, and they focus more on the problems of their organizations rather than on creative solutions that may benefit the organization and further their own growth. However, these same organizations also have some extraordinary leaders who have the entrepreneur mindset. It is these few who do wonders for their companies and grow exponentially in very little time.

All organizations obviously look for people who work with the entrepreneur mindset like leaders, rather than ordinary people with the employee mindset. So the message of this chapter really draws from its title – *The Employee Mindset vs. the Entrepreneur Mindset*. Be a leader, not just an employee of your organization or your business. A leader always works with the entrepreneur mindset and takes ownership for the organization.

Here is a true story of an employee who became a great leader owing to his entrepreneurial mindset.

In 1946, Lee Iacocca joined Ford Motors as an engineer. But he was more than just that; he was a man with an entrepreneurial mindset. Very soon he moved to the sales department, where he showed extraordinary results. He always worked as if he owned Ford Motors and so by 1960, he became the Vice President at Ford. His growth did not stop here – by 1970, he became the President at Ford Motors. How was it possible for an engineer to become the President of a giant organization like Ford Motors? It was because even though he was an employee, he always worked like a leader, with the entrepreneur mindset. He always considered Ford his own company. Interestingly, in 1978, he was fired by Henry Ford II.

Unlike an ordinary person, Iacocca did not give up. In 1979, he joined another company, called the Chrysler Corporation as President, which at that time was on the verge of bankruptcy. Soon after he joined, his performance led him to become the chairperson at Chrysler Corporation.

Iacocca's sense of ownership was evident from the efforts he made when the company was on the verge of bankruptcy; he went to the government for a loan to save Chrysler from going down, and convinced the government for a loan of $1.5 billion. Once the loan was approved, he used innovative ways with his entrepreneur mindset, to help the company be cost-effective and create better products. He also inspired his team members to function like leaders. As a result of this, in 1983, within less than five years, Chrysler repaid the loan to the government and Lee Iacocca became a national hero. This is what a person can do if he practices leadership, i.e. works with the entrepreneur mindset.

The rest of this book is a step-by-step guide for anyone who wants to develop the entrepreneur mindset and become a leader in personal and professional life. So if you are ready to awaken the leader in you, then it is time for you to do an exercise which will help you take the first step towards becoming a leader.

Exercise to awaken the leader in you

Here are some simple questions for you, which will help you determine where you stand as far as being a leader is concerned:

- What kind of person have you been working like so far: as someone with the employee mindset or with the entrepreneur mindset? (Please answer based on your current mindset and not what you wish to be).
- How exactly have you been working like someone with an employee mindset? (Please be blunt and honest with yourself; we all have the employee mindset within us).
- How exactly have you been working like a leader, with the entrepreneur mindset? (Please be kind and honest with yourself as this is also a part of you).
- Now write down how you will convert some of your employee mindset behaviours into leadership behaviours, i.e. how you will practice more of the entrepreneur mindset from now on.

All human beings have both the mindsets within them. It is the mindset we harness the most that gives us the most results – meaning that the quality of our life depends on the mindset that is pre-dominant.

Before you read any further please ensure that you answer the above questions honestly and sincerely, and I promise you that it will open up a new world of learning for you. You will realize and discover where you really need to improve and where you already practice excellence. And just to help you with this exercise, here is an example of these answers

- *What kind of person have you been working like so far?* After going through this enlightening theory of employee vs. entrepreneur mindset, I realized that I am demonstrating more of the employee mindset than the entrepreneur mindset. Although, I have been demonstrating traits from both these mindsets, I confess that I have been more of an employee than an entrepreneur!

- *How specifically have you been working with the employee mindset?*

1. Many times I don't take ownership of my work.
2. I leave work unfinished.
3. I leave for home early without finishing my work.
4. I talk to my customers rudely at times. Now I realize that it was the employee mindset at work.
5. I go late for meetings, and am not considerate of how it impacts others.
6. I crib a lot about my organizational problems with my colleagues in the cafeteria.
7. I don't keep my commitments many-a-time which affects my project deadlines.
8. I don't find new ways to get along with my managers and so I consistently have bad relationships with my bosses.
9. I take unplanned leaves without realizing how it affects the business in the long run.
10. Many times I waste the organization's resources and material by being careless about how I use them. Now I know that was behaviour which reflected my employee mindset.
11. I do only what is asked of me. I don't go out of my way to find out what else I can do to help with the project or business.
12. I don't take conscious efforts to upgrade my knowledge; rather I work on it reactively when the need arises.
13. I provide good service to my clients, but not *outstanding* service, and now I realize that if I *really* owned them as my clients, I would have delivered outstanding service.
14. I charge for the time that I spend on my services, not for the results that I create. And so many times, I don't give any kind of quality guarantee on my services. Now I realize that if I really owned my business I would not charge for my time alone, but for the actual results and in fact I would guarantee results so that more and more customers would come to my business.

- *What are the ways in which you have been working like a leader with the entrepreneur mindset?*

1. To be fair to myself, I also do behave like a leader with the entrepreneur mindset on many occasions. For example, when I go out of my way to do some things for the organization.
2. When some work is given to me, I make sure that I finish it on time, with quality.
3. When people in my team ask me for help I always co-operate, thinking their work is also a part of my work.
4. In case of failure, I don't blame anyone. Instead I take ownership and fix the problem.
5. I provide complete clarity to my team regarding on-going projects and work.
6. I ensure that confidentiality of the organization is maintained.
7. I make sure my team is happy and well-bonded.
8. I bring innovative solutions to my projects on many occasions.
9. I chose to stay with my organization when many people were leaving, and I see how I was actually employing the entrepreneur mindset at the time.
10. I am really good at what I do, because of which I have always been called to take charge during crises. I ensure I take up such opportunities as challenges.

- *Now write down how you think you will convert some of your employee mindset behaviours into leadership behaviours, i.e. how you will practice more of the entrepreneur mindset from now on.*

1. Looking at my employee mindset behaviours, I promise to immediately convert them into leadership behaviours. I will start with taking ownership of my work and leave for home when I feel I have done justice to my day of work and responsibilities.

2. I will talk to my customers assertively and make them feel special and will always be there for them sincerely.

3. I will go to meetings on time and behave like a true leader, as I want to inspire my team to do the same now.

4. I recognize there are problems in my organization, like there are in any other. But I choose to focus on the positives and strengths of my organization. After all how can I criticize my own business!

5. I will make sure that I keep my commitments so that I can contribute to my organization's success.

6. I will find new ways to get along with my managers, peers and my team, since now I feel they belong to me and are my responsibility.

7. I shall apply for leaves in advance. I shall also make sure that when I am on leave, everything is taken care of in my absence.

8. I shall use the organization's resources more carefully now on, thinking it is my own money at stake.

9. I will be proactive in finding more work when I don't have anything to work on, instead of waiting for someone to tell me what to do.

10. I shall consciously take efforts to upgrade my knowledge instead of waiting for things to become urgencies.

11. I will now provide not just good, but extraordinary service to my clients.

12. I will now charge for my results, not just for my time.

Now it is your turn to do this exercise. And if you do this exercise honestly, rest assured that a whole new world of amazing learning will open up for you and help you fulfil your goals, desires and dreams much faster than you can ever imagine!

- What kind of person have you been working like so far: as someone with the employee mindset or the entrepreneur mindset? (Please answer based on your current mindset and not what you wish to be).

- How exactly have you been working with the employee mindset? (Please be blunt and honest with yourself; this mindset is also part of your mental make-up.)
- How exactly have you been working like a leader with the entrepreneur mindset? (Please be kind and honest with yourself as this is also a part of you.)
- Now write down how you will convert some of your employee mindset behaviours into leadership behaviours, i.e. how you will practice more of the entrepreneur mindset from now on.

These answers will come handy to you, and going forward as you read on, you may want to add on to them or modify them. In the following chapters we are going to learn how to transform our mindset from the employee one to the entrepreneurial mindset in greater detail, through a more thorough understanding of the various aspects of leadership.

Chapter Summary

▶ All organizations have two kinds of people – Ordinary People who have the employee mindset and Extraordinary Leaders who work with the entrepreneur mindset.

▶ The key problem in organizations is that most people are not leaders but just ordinary employees.

▶ Be a leader not just an employee!

▶ It is *not* necessary to own a business in order to have the entrepreneur mindset. Anyone can develop this mindset and be a leader.

▶ Employees can have the entrepreneur mindset, while business owners can possess the employee mindset. It's not about whether you are in a job or run a business, it's about your mindset.

▶ Our results depend on the way we work; if we work with the employee mindset then we get ordinary results, but if we work like leaders and entrepreneurs, then we get extraordinary results.

▶ We all possess both the mindsets within us – the employee mindset as well as entrepreneurial mindset.

▶ Be aware of how you are behaving – is it like an employee or like an entrepreneur? And then commit to change your employee behaviours into entrepreneurial behaviours.

Employee Mindset
Pfizer RWD/HEOR Slides prospect
Collaterals
Home finances
Prorelationship

2

Twin Forces that Drive a Leader

I assume you have already done the exercise at the end of the first chapter, to help you understand some of your employee mindset behaviours, so that you can consciously convert them into entrepreneurial mindset behaviours. If you have not done the exercise, stop and do it now, because that is the foundation of our leadership journey.

To start with, it's time for us to dive deeper and understand the two forces that drive a leader. These two specific forces drive greatness in a leader and give him the ability to:

- Have the entrepreneur mindset
- To create extraordinary results
- To inspire people and
- To create long-lasting relationships

These twin forces are the foundations for becoming a leader, and also what differentiate a leader from an ordinary person. So if you truly want to be a leader and have the entrepreneur mindset, then your first step is to master these twin forces.

2.1

High Energy

So what do you think is the first driving force of a leader? What is the most important quality required to be a leader? I suggest you stop reading now and take a minute to think and answer this question.

During my leadership workshops when I ask this question, following are some of the answers I get from the audience:

- Most people say *vision* is the most important quality required to be a leader. I suggest here, that without the first driving force it is not possible to even create a vision.
- Some people say the first quality required is *communication*. I say that if you don't have the first driving force, you will not be able to communicate, even if you have great communication skills!
- Then some people suggest that *hard-work* is the most important quality for being a leader. But I say, that it is impossible to work hard without the first driving force because how you work depends on this driving force.
- Some people say the most important quality is that leaders must *believe* in themselves. But again, whether or not you believe in yourself, depends on the first driving force. By now people are

laughing and scratching their heads to think what *is* this driving force?!

The most common answer I finally get is *positive attitude*. And to that I say that whether your attitude is positive or negative is also determined by the first driving force.

Mostly I don't get the right answer to this question, because most of us don't realize the importance of this driving force. So here are some hints that I finally give to my audience, which I would like to share with you too. The hint is, that this driving force:

- Is always inside you and around you all the time.
- Sometimes it is high, sometimes it is medium, and sometimes it is low.
- Without this driving force there can be no life.

Now think, what can this driving force be? Even right now, this driving force is the reason that you have been able to read so far; and if this force was low for you, then you would have definitely not been able to read this far. So what do you think is this driving force?

Usually after this hint I do get the right answer and I am guessing that you have also got the right answer by now. The first driving force that differentiates a leader from ordinary people is ***High Energy.***

Leaders have high energy

Now, this may sound too simple to be true, but all profound principles in life are simple aren't they? Think about it, don't you need energy for everything in life? To create and fulfil a vision you need energy; to communicate, to listen, to respond, to think positive and to work hard also you need energy. In fact what can you do without energy?

- For example, let's say you have great communication skills, but on a day that your energy is low, are you able to communicate well? No. You can't!

- Let's say you are a very hard working person, but the day your energy is down, are you able to work hard? No. You can't!
- Think about this – sometimes you go home early and yet you are not able to spend quality time with your family. Is it because you have less time that day? No, it's because you have less energy that day.
- Yet, there are also times you go home late and still spend quality time with your family; is it because you have more time that day? Again no. It's only because you have more energy that day.

So you see *energy* is the first and foremost driving force that is required to be a leader, because without energy we cannot do anything, let alone be a leader. Ordinary people are not conscious of maintaining their energy while leaders consciously maintain high energy.

This is the reason that ordinary people always achieve less things in more time, whereas extraordinary leaders always achieve more things in less time.

But don't believe me blindly. Let's see examples of some extraordinary leaders and assess the importance of this driving force. To start with, let's talk about a man who for the first time made possible for an Indian company to be listed on the American Stock Exchange. An extraordinary leader who has accomplished so much in only 30 years, that ordinary people can only dream of achieving in a life-time.

"Infosys is a place where there is tremendous energy and enthusiasm because of the leadership."

–Narayan Murthi

You probably already know that Narayan Murthy is the founder of the biggest IT company in India, called Infosys Technologies, which he started in the year 1981. What you probably don't know, is that he started the company with a capital of a mere ₹10, 000 with six of his colleagues. His wife Sudha gave him ₹10,000 which she had saved up for a rainy day. With as small an amount as this, and a big dream, Narayan Murthy started his journey as a leader and entrepreneur and here is what he has achieved since then:

- *With his leadership, Infosys became the first Indian company to be listed on NASDAC in March 1999.*
- *In the year 2000, he was awarded the prestigious Padma Shri by the Government of India.*
- *In 2003, he was acclaimed the World Entrepreneur of the Year by Ernst and Young.*
- *He received the Padma Vibhushan award in 2008, from the Government of India.*
- *He is currently the Chairman Emeritus for Infosys.*
- *In spite of his immense responsibilities and workload, in the year 2009, he also found the time to write a book called 'A Better India, a Better World'.*

How is it, that one man was able to achieve so much in such little time? The answer is his high energy that drives him to work towards his dreams with relentless passion and zeal.

There are many people who have similar or maybe even greater dreams than Narayan Murthy, but then, why are they not able to succeed? The reason is simple: they lack the energy to learn, the energy to inspire, the energy to act, the energy to contribute, the energy to innovate, the energy to do whatever it takes to convert a dream into reality. But does this mean that people like Narayan Murthy are gifted with unlimited energy? No they are not.

The fact is that we *all* have access to unlimited energy. All we have to do, is learn to manage that energy. That's what leaders do—they learn to manage their energy.

The truth is, that *you* can also create high energy at any point of time, so that you can also achieve more things in less time. The simple and practical techniques that I am about to share with you in this chapter, will help you to create high energy whenever you want. Let me share with you the story of a great team who took advantage of these techniques and achieved extraordinary results for themselves.

I once got a call from the Director of an organization an amazing leader. He called me with a situation where his team had all the required skills, however they were low on energy because of past target failures and they were also de-motivated by the recession that had hit the world economy at the time. He realized that what his team lacked was only the energy, and so he invited me to do a two-hour session with his team, where we would train the team to generate extraordinary energy and hence extraordinary results.

In those two hours, I helped a group of 120 people to practically generate extraordinary energy and made them realize that they can achieve anything, if they maintain high energy levels at work and their personal lives. The entire group was so energized that they were willing to do whatever it took to produce the desired results in their projects, and achieve what they had thought was difficult or impossible so far.

To make sure that people really have the energy to do anything that it takes to create extraordinary results, I put them through the test of fire walking. Amazingly every single person of this group walked on fire fearlessly, because of the energy that was generated in the group. At the end of it, people were celebrating and shouting at the top of their voices with so much excitement and enthusiasm, that the session became one of the most talked about events of the year.

After this two-hour energy building and fire-walk session, in the same month, this group achieved its targets with amazing energy and enthusiasm. In the second month, they broke their target. Soon after that month, they also beat their competitors and became the best in Asia. A year after this, when I went there for a follow up

*session, I found that people were still practicing the techniques I
had shared with them to generate high energy then and were still
creating amazing results even a year after that session.*

*This story is available as a case study on my website. http://www.
miteshkhatri.com/case-studies*

Do you think this team did not have the potential to perform like this
before the session? They did, they always had the potential; they just
needed the energy to drive them to create extraordinary results for
themselves and their organization.

I am sharing these stories with you, because I want you to realize the
fact that energy is the first and the foremost driving force of leadership.
And you can learn practical ways to generate high energy for yourself
consciously.

There are many ways to generate high energy. (One of the ways of
course is to simply call me as a keynote speaker for your organization or
call me for a personal coaching session!) But you don't have to wait for
that because as promised, I will share simple and practical techniques
with you right here in this book.

Techniques to generate high energy

The rest of the chapters will continue revealing new ways of creating and
managing high energy, but here are some simple techniques to start with:

1. **Energizer games for blood circulation** – Here is a simple scientific
    principle: when we don't move, a lot our blood circulation slows
    down, which reduces the flow of blood and oxygen to our brain,
    which basically means less energy for the brain. So if you want
    more energy, you need more oxygen and blood flowing to your
    brain for which you need to move your body, and speed up your
    blood circulation.

    Do you remember how in school all our favourite teachers were
    always the ones who played with us while teaching and made it

fun? Well, they knew that the simplest way to energize children even while teaching the toughest subject, was to make them play energizing games so that they could have better blood circulation. These simple games called energizer games, are supposed to last only for two minutes but they are fun, make you laugh, make you happy and most importantly, help you re-energize yourself.

In my workshops, we follow the discipline of using a small energizing game every two hours, just to make sure that we always maintain high energy.

The amount of energy you have decides the amount of motivation you will have to create the results you want.

Thus many organizations, after my workshops have adopted this as a practice, owing to which their energy and subsequently their productivity have sky-rocketed. Just so you can see some results, here is another testimonial from an organization called GlaxoSmithKline (GSK), which got extraordinary results simply by using the technique of energizer games. You can read the entire case-study by visiting the following URL: http://www.miteshkhatri.com/case-studies/high-energy-leadership

Here are examples of some simple and effective energizer games:

a. Listen to some peppy music and dance for two minutes.
b. If you are in the office, ask your buddy/neighbour to give you a back massage for two minutes.
c. Try laughing in five different ways.
d. Think about and share your happiest experiences.
e. Make someone happy by doing something nice for them.
f. Appreciate someone for the good work they have done during the day.
g. Read some inspirational quotes on my facebook page https://www.facebook.com/MiteshKhatriPage
h. Watch some inspirational videos on my site http://www.miteshkhatri.com/videos

i   Exercise for two minutes.

j   Play cricket with a notepad and a napkin ball. (Remember you did this in school?)

k.   Play *langdi* or *pakda pakdi*.

Of course you must do these energizers based on your office environment and policies, as some of the above examples may not be possible in your organization. Be creative and come up with your own energizers which are appropriate to your environment. The idea is to make sure you are able to maintain a high level of energy at all times. Especially when you need it!

Most people underestimate the power of simplicity and because of this, might not use energizer games. But I can tell you from personal experience that even at my own workplace and with my family, I get a lot of energy by playing such games. All you have to do is keep it simple, keep it short (approximately for two minutes), make sure it moves your body to get your blood circulation going, and that it makes you happy!

2. **Love what you do** – Now this second technique is one that all, and I mean *all* the leaders in the world use; but this technique is also highly misunderstood. So when I say 'love what you do', people think they need to find their dream job before they love doing what they do. On the contrary, this technique is about loving whatever you do – without judging it or demeaning it. Do you remember how Dhoni used to be a Train Ticket Examiner? I am sure he did that job with as much passion then, as he does now as captain of the Indian cricket team. Changing jobs will never change who you are, but who you are will definitely change your job experience.

    I see a lot of people cribbing about their work profiles and feeling small about their work, and every time in my workshops I remind them that if you love what you do, you will attract the work that you love. But if you hate what you do today, you will never find the job you love tomorrow, because you won't have the energy to create the results required for it.

Gandhiji was a great leader and yet he never felt ashamed to clean his own toilet. The message Gandhiji was giving out was that whatever you do, you must do it with love. Imagine if for one single day of your life you would love doing whatever you had to, without any complaints. Just love everything you do for one day. Imagine how amazing your day would be!

What if you did your work with love even if your domestic help did not come in the morning? What if you did your work with love even if your colleagues were not there to support you on a difficult task? What if you did your work with love even if you had to stay back late in the office? What if you did your work with love even if you had to come home and play with your children and help them with their homework? It's late night, you are tired, but your spouse wants to spend some time with you, what if you did that with love?

Many people do all of these things, but they do them with irritation, complaints and resistance. But the point is, if you are going to do it anyway, why not do it with love? Because when you do the same work without loving it, you lose energy and feel drained. And when you do the same things with love, you find yourself full of energy, and even people around you get affected by your energy.

So to start with, write down all the areas in which you think you are working *without* love, and then choose to do them *with* love. Like I mentioned before, you have anyway been doing these things for so long your way, now for just one day, try doing these same things with love.

Do it like you are an artist; do it like you are in love with it; do it like it is your passion; and do it like it is your greatest opportunity to make a difference! I promise you, if you do this for one day, you will have such abundance of energy, that you will finish much more work than you have on any other day. And the best part would be that at the end of the day you will not be tired, but full of energy. Sounds good huh? So let's start the exercise using this table below:

Things I do daily, but not with love	How I now choose to do these with love

3. **Change what you can and accept what you can't** – Leaders are masters at using this technique and so are able to remain energized even during the most stressful situations, both at work and at home.

   Leaders understand that there are things and people in life who can be changed, and then there are things and people who cannot be changed. They are smart and know how to work with things and people that can change. They also quickly accept things and people who cannot change; in this way they never waste their energy.

   Ordinary people struggle with things and people they cannot change; they keep fighting, pushing and working hard at them. It is because of this that ordinary people waste a lot of energy and then they have hardly any energy left for the things and people that they actually can change.

   Have you ever imagined how the heads of countries handle the amount of stress that they have to deal with? They are able to deal with it because they are quick to accept things and people who cannot change, and then re-focus all their energies only on things and people who can change.

   That's how extraordinary leaders maintain their high energy levels; they invest it in the right places. When I do this exercise during my leadership workshops, I have CEOs telling me that literally 50% of their stress has dropped and that they have regained a lot of energy because of this technique alone.

Try it out for yourself by using this table where you identify all the things and people you are struggling with. Then identify whether they can be changed or not. Depending on that answer, choose to either continue working on them, or accept them fully. I bet when you do this exercise you will find many things and people on whom you are wasting your energy, which you could have re-focused on other things and people and got some real results. Here are a couple of examples to get you started:

Things and people I am struggling with	Can they be changed or not	Will you continue working on them or accept them
My boss	No	Accept
My subordinate	Yes	Continue working on

4. **Sleep well** – All computers need to be switched off regularly to help them work at their optimum level. Similarly, all human minds need to shut down regularly, to help them work at their optimum potential. All ordinary people take sleep for granted, while leaders use sleep to re-energize themselves completely.

You will see most people don't sleep well, due to which their minds hardly get time to reboot completely. So in the mornings they find themselves low on energy and sluggish, just like a slow computer. This affects the entire day negatively, and makes it difficult to deal with the kind of pressures we are facing in the 21st century. We must let our brain shut down completely by sleeping well, so that it helps us to be fully energized.

Here is a little scientific information that will help you

understand the importance of sleep. We all have a conscious and a subconscious mind. While the subconscious mind has unlimited capacity to store information, the conscious mind has very limited capacity.

When we work during the day, we use up all the capacity of the conscious mind and consume all our energy, due to which we naturally feel tired in the evenings. At night when you sleep, and if you sleep well, all the information in your conscious mind gets downloaded to your subconscious mind. Your subconscious mind keeps all this information stored, to be used when necessary.

If you sleep long enough and deep enough, you allow this download process to complete, due to which the conscious mind is ready to be used with its full capacity again the next morning, making you feel fresh and energized.

But if you sleep less, or if you sleep disturbed, then you don't allow the conscious mind to download and empty all the information to the subconscious mind. It is because of this, that you get up in the morning feeling tired and sluggish.

Let's say that one night you don't sleep well; you interrupt this download process. So when you wake up, your conscious mind still has 30% information still eating up its memory and making you feel tired. Now you work the whole day and gather 100% more information in your conscious mind, and thus feel extremely tired at the end of the day because now you have 30+100=130% information i.e. 30% more information than your conscious mind can handle.

Again that night you don't sleep well and the download process does not complete. So when you get up in the morning, you now have 60% information eating into your conscious mind's memory, making you even more tired the next morning. But you work the whole day again, gathering another 100% work information, which at the end of the day is now a total of 160% in your conscious mind. Imagine how tired you would feel if this cycle goes on for a week!

If I am not wrong, you have probably at some time or the other experienced an overload in your conscious mind because of the lack of quality and adequate amount of sleep. Then I am sure you understand that this way you will only lose more and more energy, and become increasingly un-productive every day.

In the long run, this will result in health issues like headaches, blood pressure, heart problems, and the like which will further damage your immune system. I don't mean to scare you, but only share the truth.

In fact here is the good news: now that you know how to deal with this problem, prioritize your sleep; shut your brain down completely at night. This way it will get enough time to download all the information to your subconscious mind and you will get up completely fresh and energized! Here are some simple steps to follow to sleep well at night.

a. **Sleep fresh to get up fresh** – Have a bath or wash your hands, legs and face with cold or luke warm water. Why is this important? Because you have to make sure you don't sleep too tired, because then the brain does not have enough energy to even start the download process. So make sure you freshen up with a quick bath, or at least wash your hands, legs and face with cold water to feel fresh just before you sleep.

b. **Forgiveness and gratitude** – We have a lot of anger, resentment and negative emotions from a lot of things that may have happened during the day. This interferes with the download process because sleep gets disturbed. So before you sleep, make peace with the world and yourself. Let go of the anger and remember to thank the universe for the good things that have happened that day.

All leaders are known to remember the best things of their lives or the day before they sleep, while all ordinary people focus on the worst things that happened, before they fall asleep.

So be a leader and adopt this simple technique to maintain your energy levels to sleep well.

Sleep straight on your back, take a few deep breaths and say these statements to yourself: 'I am sleeping peacefully forgiving anything wrong that happened today and feeling grateful for everything good that happened today. When I wake up in the morning, I will be completely fresh and awake, ready to start my day with lots of energy'. These simple steps will help you sleep really well and help you wake up with a lot of energy.

In the next chapter, I shall share the second driving force of leaders. But until then, you must practice the techniques given in this chapter to create high energy and take the first step to awaken the leader in you.

Chapter Summary

▶ There are two forces that drive greatness in leaders.
▶ These forces are the foundation for becoming a leader and developing the entrepreneur mindset.
▶ The first driving force of a leader is High Energy.
▶ It is high energy that gives leaders the ability to achieve more in less time.
▶ All of us have unlimited energy and potential.
▶ Energy helps release the unlimited potential that is within all of us.
▶ The amount of your energy decides the amount of your motivation.
▶ Energizer games are great for blood circulation, which revitalize mind and body.
▶ Love what you do.
▶ Change what you can; accept what you can't.
▶ Sleep well: shut down your brain completely to wake up fresh and re-energized.
▶ The next chapter explains the second driving force in detail.

2.2

―――――――――――◦⊃⊂⊃⊂◦―――――――――――

The Higher the Leader, the Higher the Expectations

"Be the change you want to see in the world."
— Mahatma Gandhi

So by now it is established that in order to be an extraordinary leader, you must transform your mindset from the employee mindset to the entrepreneur mindset. As discussed in the previous chapter, the first step to do that is to work on your energy levels; because if you don't have the ability to manage high energy then you won't have the capacity to perform like a leader. (I hope you have implemented the techniques given in the previous chapters to help you create high energy at any point of time. Remember energy is the first and foremost pre-requisite.)

Now that you have the first driving force of energy, you are ready to learn about the second driving force of a leader which makes him *extraordinary*. This is the driving force that gives leaders access to unlimited energy to work on their goals and achieve them.

I know you would be excited to know what the second driving force is; so let's get started with a simple guessing game:

There are two things in life: desires and expectations. Which do you think are stronger? Are desires stronger, or expectations?

I have been asking this question for many years now in my leadership workshops. And I have asked this question to more than 50,000 people and almost always, I get the answer that desires are stronger. If your answer is the same, then here is a question I would like to ask you:

Whether you work for some company or your own *Do you get your salary every month?*

Hopefully like most people, your answer is 'yes', you do get your salary every month. In that case, an even more important question is:

What if you don't get your salary next month? What will you do?

Now I know this may not be a very pleasant question, but please try answering it.

So again, what if you don't get your salary next month? What will you do?

Probably you will make some noise in the Human Resource department and wait for another month or two, but **eventually if you don't get your salary what will you do?**

My gut feeling is, you would do what any ordinary person would do. That is, look for another job where you would get the salary for the hard work that you put in every month. This is totally understandable and justified.

Now here is the most important question: *Is your salary just a desire, or a basic expectation?*

I am sure your salary is not just a desire, it is your expectation to get your salary every month, right?

Assuming your answer is 'yes', your salary is an expectation for you, would you ever give up on your salary?

No, I am sure you would not. You would make sure you get it either from your current employer, or some other employer. But you will make sure you get your salary when that is what you are working for.

So you see, your salary is your *expectation* and you will never give up on it. This shows us something really amazing about human behaviour and that is:

People may or may not give up on their desires, but they never give up on their expectations!

There are times when people give up on their desires, but they never give up on what they truly expect. So what are stronger desires or expectations? The answer is colon, expectations.

High expectations give high energy to leaders

Many people have dreams and desires, but until those desires become their expectations, they never have the unlimited energy to make it happen. This is the second driving force of a leader – the ability to have high expectations and not just desires.

Let's understand this more in depth. Let's understand why expectations are stronger than desires the language we use for desires is when we say 'we should' do something; while the language we use for expectations is when we say 'we must' do something.

A typical example is that most people desire to exercise every day to keep healthy, and yet most people don't have the energy to exercise every day because they think they 'should' exercise. When you desire something and you think you 'should' do it, you don't have the unlimited energy to create extraordinary results, because it is not a 'must'.

Should vs Must

'Should' is a very weak desire with no conviction in it. Just like when people say: 'I know I should exercise and lose weight' – it's a weak desire and thus, they are not willing to go to *any* extent to make it happen. They therefore don't get the energy to work on it.

Here is a list of common desires that people have in their 'should' list:

1. I know I *should* eat healthy food.
2. I know I *should* not overeat.
3. I know I *should* upgrade my knowledge and skills.
4. I know I *should* improve my communication.
5. I know I *should* find a better job.

6. I know I *should* learn to make my relationship better.
7. I know I *should* be more committed at work/home.
8. I know I *should* not shout at people.
9. I know I *should* develop patience.
10. I know I *should* read more or attend more workshops to grow.

When people say something 'should' happen, it also means its fine if it does *not* happen. Their minds say *chalta hai*. It is not a matter of life and death for them. Well obviously, if it is not that important then they will never make it happen. This is the mindset of all ordinary people and that's why they are ordinary, because they have weak desires.

On the other hand, there are extraordinary people who convert their desires into high expectations. They decide to make it a 'must' to attain them, not just a 'should'. They decide to make it a matter of life and death. It's not acceptable to them if they don't get what they want, it's not ok – *Chalta hai, nahi chalega!*

These people are known as extraordinary leaders because they take their desires and convert them into high expectations and make it an absolute 'must' for themselves. This is where they get their source of unlimited energy to make things happen.

Think about it, when something is a 'must' for you, if it is a matter of life and death, will you have the energy to make it happen? I bet you will. Here is how leaders talk about their desires which are converted into clear expectations:

1. I *must* exercise every day and keep fit.
2. I *must* meet all my commitment and delivery timelines.
3. I *must* reach on time anywhere and everywhere.
4. My team *must* perform and create results.
5. I *must* maintain my weight and be healthy.
6. I *must* have a great relationship.
7. I *must* improve my communication.
8. I *must* have great results in my job.

9. I *must* not shout at people.
10. I *must* learn to be assertive with people.
11. I *must* have patience.
12. I *must* upgrade my knowledge and skills regularly.

Leaders never settle for less than their expectations, because they believe they deserve the best and are willing to work for it. When we make something a 'must', then we go to any extent to make things happen.

Let's say God forbid, if your child needs urgent medical treatment and you need to arrange ₹50 lakhs for an operation in just two days, or he won't survive. In this case, would you make sure that you arrange the money within two days? I am sure your answer is 'yes'. You would arrange the money because this is not something you think you *should* do, it is something you think you *must* do.

When things become 'musts' for human beings, it gives them unlimited energy to achieve what they want.

Another simple example is if you simply desire that your team 'should' perform at extraordinary levels, will they? Well they *may* or *may not*!

But what if you have high expectations, and if you say it is a *must* for your team to perform at extraordinary levels, then will they? Absolutely!

You would make sure your team performs extraordinarily because it is a *must* for you. You will not wait for the right conditions, the right time, right project or the right people. You would not even wait for God! You will make it happen because it's a must!

High Expectations (Must a Source of Unlimited Energy) ⇨ High Results (Since it is a Must)

High Expectations Lead to High Results

Think of this if you had two bosses, one who has high expectations of you and the other who has low expectations of you, who would make you grow faster – the boss who expects more or the one who expects less?

The boss who has high expectations of you, would be the one to make you grow faster, wouldn't he?

Steve Jobs of Apple is a great example of someone who always created extraordinary results. This was because he always expected very high results from his team at Apple. He had this amazing ability to have such high expectations, that he would make it an absolute must for people to create extraordinary results, as if it were a matter of life and death. People said it was not easy to satisfy him, obviously, because he had very high expectations and very high standards. That is why he is greatly missed. It is indeed difficult to replace someone with such high expectations and standards.

Here is another story of an exceptional entrepreneur who is also one of the youngest and most extraordinary leaders in the world today.

On the 4th of February 2004, a young 19 year old entrepreneur started a business and in just four years, he had become one of the youngest self-made billionaire at the age of 23. In 2010, Vanity Fair magazine put him at number one on their list of the top 100 "Most Influential People of the Information Age". Almost the whole world is now on his social media site. Probably you too are on his website – Facebook.

Mark Zuckerberg, *the founder of Facebook, is someone I truly admire for his energy and his high expectations. Success is certainly not a mere 'should' when it comes to Zuckerberg; it's* *a 'must' for him. One of the examples of how highly he expects from his team at Facebook, is an event which he has every six to eight weeks called the "hackathon", where he inspires his team to think of a new project and complete it in a single night. They are expected to think of a new idea and take it to the level of successful completion in just one night; now that is very high expectation.*

Even today, Facebook is adding so much value to its customers with new applications and features, that it seems almost impossible for any competitor to beat it. No organization can perform so well without the leader expecting a lot from the team and pushing it to get results.

Let's do a small recap here: High expectations or the 'must' attitude is the driving force that gives leaders unlimited energy to create extraordinary results in life.

In fact **the higher the expectations, the higher will be the performance.**

But there is one small problem here what happens when someone expects very highly from you? How do you feel? For example, if you are used to getting up at 7 am and now if someone expects you to get up every morning at 5 am, how would you feel?

I am sure your answer is the same as I am thinking. Pressure! It is natural for human beings to feel pressure when someone expects highly from us. And the moment we feel pressure, what do we naturally do? Do we naturally move towards pressure or move away from it?

Naturally most people move away from pressure, and the moment you move away from pressure what are you moving away from? Obviously along with pressure you move away from expectations, which is creating that pressure and in turn you are also moving away from performance.

This is the problem about expectations that I wanted to bring to your notice.

High expectations will lead to high performance, but before that they will also always create high pressure, and most people try to avoid pressure due to which they can never manage high expectations and thus cannot have extraordinary results!

For example, if your boss or your client starts expecting more than what you are delivering, then it is natural for you to feel a lot of pressure. But if you avoid that pressure, you would not only avoid their expectations, but also fail to create extraordinary performance because you limit yourself and hence do not grow.

So is pressure necessary for growth? Yes, absolutely. Pressure is necessary for growth because it is a natural part of high expectations.

If you go to the gym and don't take the pressure to increase the amount of time you spend exercising, then you will never increase your stamina and strength. Thus, we must learn to take high pressure and deal with it willingly, rather than avoid it. Leadership is all about high expectations and it comes along with an equally high amount of pressure.

The level of pressure that you can handle will decide the level of leadership that you can achieve. People like Mahatma Gandhi, Narayan Murthy, Steve Jobs, Mark Zuckerberg and many great leaders like them went through huge amounts of pressure because of high expectations. But they made sure they dealt with the pressure; they did not avoid it and that's what made them such great leaders.

Leaders know that high expectations will lead to high pressure, but that they will also lead to high results. The quality of your life will depend on the amount of pressure you can handle. So if you truly want to have an extraordinary life then you must learn to deal with pressure. In fact the more pressure you are willing to deal with, the better results you will see in your life.

When you move to a higher position in your career, the pressure increases, but along with that your salary, your power, your influence, your authority, your privileges also increase, don't they? The top management usually gets the highest salary, power, influence, authority and privileges, because they are the ones who are handling the maximum amount of pressure. So you see, high expectations lead to high pressure but they also lead to higher results.

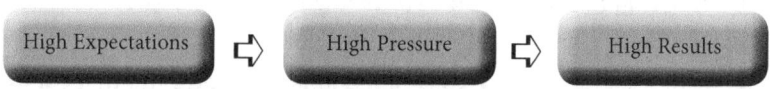

The Inevitable Cycle: The Higher the Expectations, the Higher the Pressure and the Results

Even in relationships, couples start facing the real pressure only after marriage. It is after marriage that expectations increase and subsequently the pressure increases alongside. Those who avoid this pressure and don't deal with it, eventually destroy their marriage. Those who learn to deal with this pressure, create extraordinary relationships and convert conflicts into great learning experiences. If you truly expect to have a great relationship with your partner, then find a way to deal with the pressure during conflict situations, and re-create trust and love in your relationship.

So are you ready to be a to leader and to create an entrepreneur mindset? If you are, then you must also be ready to go through high pressure. I promise that if you learn to deal with high expectations and pressure, you will definitely be an extraordinary leader who will become an example for people around.

If you are ready to face high expectations and pressure, then let's start with this exercise here. This is a brilliant exercise which will help you to recognize areas in which you have weak desires, and you have the choice to convert them into clear expectations. Just be honest with yourself and answer these questions:

- *What are the desires that you have been struggling to realize?* By struggle I mean, that you haven't been getting the results you want. Either you don't get the time, or you don't have the energy or the motivation or the resources for working towards it. Examples of these desires may be fitness, weight loss, learning something new, getting a new job, getting a promotion, buying a house, making a savings plan or any other goal. *What are the pressures you are trying to avoid in working towards these desires?*

- Are these desires 'shoulds' or 'musts' for you?
- If they are 'musts', are you willing to face the pressure that comes along with them?
- If yes, then write down the pressures you are willing to face.
- Now declare that from now onwards these are not just desires, but clear expectations from yourself; they are absolute musts for you and you are not ok living your life without achieving these goals.

The following table will help you do this exercise. All you have to do is be honest with yourself:

List of desires	Pressure that you are avoiding	Is this a should or a must for you? Desire or Expectation?	Pressures that you are willing to face for it	Declaration of this as a must for you

Once you are clear with your expectations and the pressures you would be facing, this clarity will give you unlimited energy and power to create extraordinary results. Please do this exercise and do email me your results at mitesh@guidinglightindia.com. I would love to be a part of your leadership journey.

In the following chapters, you will learn innovative ways of harnessing these two forces of high energy and high expectations. You will also learn effective ways of dealing with pressure and thus create inspiring results in your life. Until then, all the best and expect high things from yourself this week. Be a leader.

Chapter Summary

▶ Human beings have desires and they also have expectations.

▶ People may or may not give up on their desires, but they *never* give up on their expectations.

▶ Thus expectations are stronger than desires.

▶ The second driving force of a leader is to have High Expectations.

▶ High expectations give leaders access to unlimited energy.

▶ The term used for desires is 'I *should* do it'.

▶ The term used for high expectations is "I *must* do it".

▶ When we use the word 'should' it means it's ok if things don't happen.

▶ When we use the word 'must', it's a matter of life and death.

▶ 'Should' does not have enough energy to make things happen.

▶ 'Must' has unlimited energy to make things happen.

▶ High expectations lead to high pressure and high performance.

▶ It is natural for ordinary people to avoid pressure, instead of dealing with it.

▶ But when they avoid pressure, they also avoid high expectations and high performance.

▶ Leaders deal with high expectations and pressure; they don't avoid them.

▶ Pressure is necessary for growth.

▶ The quality of your life will depend on the amount of pressure you can handle.

3

The Source of Power and Energy – Taking 100% Responsibility

I have always been obsessed with understanding the difference between ordinary and extraordinary people? In fact, ask yourself the following very intriguing questions:

- I want you to think, why is it that some people are negatively impacted by crises, while others are able to convert crises into opportunities?
- Why is it that some people lose control during conflicts, while others end up taking control?
- Have you ever asked yourself, what the difference between these kinds of people is?
- Why do some people become weak in difficult situations, while others become stronger?
- How come some people get tired owing to heavy work, while others maintain their energy levels?

I promised you in the second chapter that I would share with you many secrets of what gives unlimited energy to leaders. So here is another secret to their unlimited power and energy.

Taking 100% responsibility – a source of unlimited power and energy.

Leaders take 100% responsibility for their life situations. I am sure you would agree that leaders don't blame or complain; they simply take responsibility for their situations, problems, relationships, conflicts – for everything. This is another secret to their unlimited power and energy.

The bottom line is, to be an extraordinary leader one needs to stop blaming and complaining. Blaming people, situations, luck, parents, teams, peers, line managers, management, market conditions, weather, money, spouse, children and so on, must stop and instead, 100% responsibility for everything must be taken. Ordinary people blame and complain, while leaders take responsibility to change their results.

A lot of people tell me that it's not easy to take responsibility all the time. I won't be surprised if you are thinking the same as you read this. In fact I would also agree that it is really not easy to be responsible all the time. However, if one is to be extraordinary, one also has to dare to do what extraordinary leaders do, and stop doing what ordinary people do.

Here are some statements, I share in my workshops to urge people to stop indulging in the futile activity of blaming and complaining:

- Even if you don't have the right boss
- You did not get the expected results in your appraisals
- Your spouse does not get along with you
- Your team is not performing
- Your people don't listen to you
- Someone else is stopping you from growing

Whenever I make such statements, a very common question is asked by many participants, and I won't be surprised if you have the same question in your mind right now. The question is: *'So do I accept things the way they are even when things are going wrong? Do I accept people the way they are even when they are doing the wrong things?'*

No, absolutely not! Leadership is not about avoiding the wrong things or people, and it is definitely not about accepting low standards. On the contrary, leadership is about doing the right thing, even when it seems difficult. But here is the important part: when you are in a state of blame and complain, do you really think you can do the right thing? Do you really think you can use the best of your intelligence? Certainly, the answer is no.

There is actually a lot of power in taking responsibility. When you take responsibility, it also means you are in control. And being in control is synonymous with being in power. Very few people understand the relationship between responsibility and power; leaders do. On the contrary, you will only lose power and energy by blaming and complaining.

A lot of people ask, how can one not feel bad when let's say, they are not supported by significant people in their lives? They ask, 'Is it not natural to feel bad when you don't get what you expect, or what you think you deserve?' My answer to these questions is that it is natural to feel bad, but it certainly isn't natural to blame and complain.

It must be realized that blaming and complaining are limiting and debilitating factors which make people weak, not strong. The act of blaming and complaining also takes up a lot of time and energy which otherwise could have been invested in much more fruitful activities. Taking 100% responsibility means you own your life completely, like an entrepreneur who owns his business and takes responsibility to solve problems rather than blaming and complaining.

Taking responsibility for yourself, your life and every situation starts with asking yourself some basic questions like:

- What part did I play in the way things are happening in my life?
- How can I change what is happening?
- What changes can I make in myself to change my environment?
- How can I change to change my results?

Here is an amazing story of a leader who took responsibility instead of blaming and complaining.

You have probably heard of Virgin Airlines, UK, which was founded by the entrepreneur Richard Branson. Here is his fascinating story:

He was once stuck at an airport with his wife because his flight was cancelled. There were hundreds of people in the same situation, who were angry and frustrated as it is considered natural to feel so. But Richard Branson had the innate qualities of a leader, and with his entrepreneur mindset he started thinking of how he could take responsibility for the situation he was in, and take the next flight to Puerto Rico, which is where he wanted to go.

Here is what he did: He made a few calls to some charter companies and checked to charter a plane for $2000. He calculated the number of seats in the plane and divided it by $2000 and this gave him a great idea. He made a placard that said: 'Virgin Airlines: $39 Single Flight to Puerto Rico' and walked around with this placard on the airport where many people were sitting, frustrated and waiting.

In a little while, he had sold all the seats on the flight leaving two for himself and his wife. This way he got himself to Puerto Rico in his own chartered plane, and even helped many others to get to their destination. That was the start of Virgin Airlines (although it was formally launched in 1984) which happened because one person chose to take responsibility for his situation, instead of blaming and complaining.

But does that mean, that next time your flight is delayed you too must hire a chartered plane and do what Richard Branson did? No! He did what he thought was right in his situation, you do what you think is right in your situation.

One of my dear friends called Nityashanti, was recently stuck at the airport, so he decided that instead of blaming and complaining, he would use this time to count his blessings and feel gratitude for all the things that he has in life. This way he took responsibility for his situation in his own unique manner.

So the key is ownership. One has to own the situation and take responsibility for it – not spend time and energy cribbing and complaining. So for instance, if you don't get along with your boss, then own this problem and take responsibility by doing something to improve your relationship with him. The action can be anything – having a conversation with your boss, changing jobs, or simply improving your performance to the level expected, so that your boss changes his attitude towards you; or maybe you could learn a new way to communicate with your boss. Do anything, but *do something* to take full responsibility of the problem and solve the problem. If you did not get the expected results in your appraisals, instead of cribbing about it in the cafeteria, take responsibility and do something about it. Have a detailed discussion with your boss; understand where you might have gone wrong; negotiate with your boss effectively; find new ways of upgrading your value in the organization, so that they are compelled to give you the results you expect the next time. If your life partner does not get along with you, then learn new ways of influencing and communicating in a way that will compel your partner to get along with you. Do whatever it takes and take 100% responsibility and own the situation instead of blaming and complaining about your partner.

The ability to take responsibility is the ability to respond to situations in a way that gives you results; that gives you what *you* want. The ability to take responsibility means you completely own the problem because it's your business and in your business you are the one who owns everything, the success and failure both. The moment you start looking at everything in your life as *your* business and start taking responsibility of your problems and situations, you will be able to create results of your choice; and that's how you become a leader.

Leaders have an edge over ordinary people because they take 100% responsibility of their lives. They take complete ownership of their situations. This is how they create the entrepreneur mindset and create extraordinary results. This is their secret to unlimited power and energy. But people frequently ask me: *Is there a formula to be more responsible and hence be successful?'* Yes, fortunately there is a formula!

The Responsibility Formula

The Responsibility Formula (RF) used by leaders to get guaranteed success is:

(S) Situation + (R) Response = (Re) Results

S + R = Re

Whenever a Situation (S) occurs in which you are not happy with the results, change your Response (R) to it and thus change your Results (Re). Here are some case studies to show you how leaders use the Responsibility Formula.

This is a company which almost every child in India loves. It is an organization, which rules the market share by over 70% and dominates all its competitors. The organization I am talking about is **Cadbury.**

India's favorite chocolate manufacturer Cadbury, was facing a big crisis in October 2003, when some customers reported finding worms in their chocolates, and the Maharashtra Food and Drug Administration (FDA) immediately seized all their stocks at their Pune plant. As a result of this incident, their sales immediately dropped by 30% and they started losing business rapidly.

What did they do? Did they start blaming and complaining? Or did they take responsibility? Cadbury being a market leader behaved exactly like a leader would, and took responsibility to change their results.

This was a (S) Situation, where instead of blaming and complaining, they (R) Responded differently to change their (Re) Results. Under the leadership of their MD Bharat Puri, they took ownership and responded by creating a project called "Vishwas" to tackle this problem. They invested ₹15 crores on imported machinery for better packaging of their chocolates and in just four months, they re-launched Cadbury chocolates in a new packaging and even increased their advertisement budgets by 10-15%. They also hired a new brand ambassador – Amitabh Bachchan, to use his credibility to do some heavy endorsement in order to regain the trust of their customers.

In just six months after that, Cadbury regained over 70% of the market share in the chocolate industry. (You can read the full story here: http://www.rediff.com/money/2006/dec/24cad.htm) This is what I call leadership. No wonder Cadbury is still one of the leading chocolate brands in India.

On similar lines, is the example of the Indian actor Amitabh Bachchan, who went through extremely difficult situations but just because he (R) Responded differently to his (S) Situation he was able to change his (R) Results.

Amitabh Bachchan is one of the leading names of Indian cinema. Did he use the Responsibility Formula of S + R = Re to get where he did? Read on to know...

Amitabh Bachchan was faced with the (S) Situation of losing millions of rupees through his production company ABCL, and was looking at a near-hopeless financial collapse. Ordinary people in this situation would have given up, perhaps blamed others; many also would have also complained and blamed their destiny.

He however, was not to be one of them. He took ownership

and (R) Responded differently by taking corrective actions. He started working harder by signing more movies than he otherwise would have, just to pay off his debts. In fact he also signed a television show and hosted the path breaking quiz show "Kaun Banega Crorepati", even though it was against the popular wisdom of the time. He followed this up by endorsing different brands and products across the board, and did everything possible to take complete responsibility to change his (R) Results.

Within five years, he had not only recovered from his financial crisis, but was also in his second innings as one of India's most loved, successful and best paid actors. With such a turnaround, he has now become a legend in the world of entertainment and branding, not only in but internationally also.

You too can be the master of your own destiny if you master the formula of S + R = Re. I can keep giving you examples of how fool-proof the RF formula is. But the one feature common to every example is that all these people who succeeded, always took responsibility for their situations, they did not blame and complain and that's what gave them the unlimited power and energy to change and create their desired results.

Remember: blaming and complaining makes you a victim, whereas taking 100% responsibility for your life empowers you and makes you a leader. What do you choose to be – the victim or a leader?

Here is a story that I can never forget. I once met a woman who was working as senior manager for a well-reputed company. She had been successful professionally and was at the peak of her career. However, her husband now wanted her to quit and become a housewife. However, she wanted to work and continue making a mark professionally.

When she met me she was undergoing a lot of stress because of the situation and was feeling extremely hostile towards her husband.

She attended my workshop, and realized that ultimately she was the one responsible for her life and the situation she was in. It was she, who had chosen to marry her husband. She realized that she had never shared with him how ambitious she was about her career.

She did not set the right expectations with him. She saw that the only thing for her now, was to stop playing victim and instead, take responsibility. Blaming and complaining would not help her get anywhere.

She understood the equation of S + R = Re, and decided to take 100% responsibility for her life. She asked me: "How can I communicate with my husband for him to understand how I really feel and allow me to continue working?" Now this was a question coming from a leader, not from a victim.

By asking this question, she had completely re-oriented her focus from blame and complain, to action and response. Our entire focus changes when we are willing to take responsibility for our lives. I helped her build on her communication skills so that she could respond to this situation differently. She learnt new ways of communication with which she approached her husband. This created magical results in mere two hours of communication. They decided that she would continue working, but that she would also make sure that she comes home on time, even though it meant she would have to make some sacrifices at work. They also decided that on weekends she would give her complete attention to her family and would not attend to any office work. This is the compromise that the couple arrived at, which became possible only once she took complete responsibility of her life-situation and gave up blaming and complaining.

She changed her response to the situation and hence got the results that she wanted, by using the Responsibility Formula. How did she create this magic and become such an influential communicator? Well, she went through my leadership workshop where she learnt these skills in detail. I will share some of these important skills of communication with you in chapter 9.

In the meantime, I would urge you to focus on what this chapter had to say about taking 100% responsibility for your life and actions, thus gaining unlimited power and energy. Remember, you have to be a leader and not a victim. Below are some sample situations for you to practice the Responsibility Formula.

For the following situations write down how you will respond. Remember, the option of blaming and complaining does not exist.

Situation #1 – You had committed a date to your client for the delivery of a project. However, you will not able to meet the deadline now, since one of your colleagues has not done his part of the work on time. How will you respond to this situation without blaming and complaining?

Your Response

_____

_____

_____

_____

_____

_____

_____

_____

Situation #2 – You get a salary hike, but not the expected promotion in your appraisal. How will you respond to this situation by not blaming and complaining?

Your Response

_____

_____

_____

_____

_____

_____

Situation #3 – Your children are not listening to you and not taking time out to study. How will you respond to this situation in a manner that does not involve you blaming your children or complaining about them?

Your Response

_____

_____

_____

_____

_____

Situation #4 – You are the director of your company and realize that your fellow directors do not respect you and do not value your opinion. How will you respond to this situation differently instead of getting into a conflict situation and blaming your peers or complaining to/about them?

Your Response

_____

_____

_____

_____

_____

Situation #5 – Your subordinate is not doing his work with the expected quality. This person has also got into the habit of making excuses. How will you respond to this situation without accusing the person or complaining about him?

Your Response

_____

_____

_____

_____

_____

_____

_____

Once you do these exercises, your mind will get tuned to thinking differently. It will result in your mind being stretched to think differently, to take responsibility. This next exercise is going to be particularly valuable for you.

Now that you have practiced to go beyond blaming and complaining, think and make a note of five situations from your own life where you are blaming and complaining right now, and think of ways in which you can take responsibility for them.

Responsibility Questions

Another practice that will help you take 100% responsibility in your life, is getting into the habit of asking yourself what I term as 'Responsibility Questions'. This is the process of asking and answering questions in your mind. However, these are different from questions which lead you to blaming and complaining. Some examples of questions that lead to blaming and complaining are:

- Why is this happening to me?
- Why do they behave like this?
- Why can't they leave me alone?
- How can I not be upset when they behave like this?
- Why is luck not in my favour?
- Why can't my boss be more understanding?
- Why do I meet people like this every time?
- Why can't people understand what I am saying?
- Why do I have to change every time? Why can't they change?
- Why doesn't my team listen to me?

When you ask yourself questions like these, you only get responses which lead you to blame and complain about your situation and people. If you ask your mind, 'Why am I so fat?' your mind will say: 'Because you deserve to be fat!' When you ask yourself negative questions, you get negative answers. So if you ask yourself questions which seek to blame others, the result will never be positive or action-oriented. The answer will only be a complaint about the situation or people. For example, if you ask yourself: 'Why does my boss keep troubling me?' Your mind will answer – 'Because he doesn't like me, or because he hates me, or because he wants me to resign'. The danger in asking these kinds of negative questions is that they foster even more negativity and ultimately affect your personality, speech, actions and inculcate the employee mindset.

Leaders are always conscious of the questions they ask themselves.

That's what helps them take 100% responsibility for their life and practice the entrepreneur mindset. Following are the sort of questions leaders ask themselves, as they are seeking to look for solutions and ways in which they can improve upon the situation:

- What about me created this situation?
- What have I not done, which I should have done?
- How can I change what is happening?
- How can I influence their behaviour?
- How can I make sure they listen?
- How can I make them perform?
- How can I make friends instead of enemies here?
- How do I make them realize that I am on their side?
- What can I learn from this situation?
- How can I interpret this more positively?
- What is good about this situation?
- What is stopping me from getting what I want?
- What is the intention of my communication?
- How would I like my team to perform at the end of this year?
- How will my actions and reactions impact people around me?

These kind of powerful responsibility questions, will help you think in a responsible manner and help you respond differently to situations in life. If you ask yourself questions that foster responsibility, your mind will give you answers that are oriented towards more responsibility. Ultimately this affects your entrepreneur mindset. In fact you can even help other people become responsible by asking them responsibility questions. The American President Kennedy once said: 'Ask not what your country can do for you, ask what you can do for your country.' By asking this question he changed the way people thought, and helped them take responsibility.

Write down some of the questions that can help you take 100% responsibility for some of the current challenges in your life:

- Health challenges.
- Family challenges.
- Professional challenges.
- Relationship challenges.
- Conflict situations.
- Money situations.

The more you master the skill of asking yourself responsibility questions, the more positive solutions you will get from your mind. The extent to which you have control of your life depends on the extent to which you can take responsibility

In the next chapter we shall learn about how leaders command respect, and why everyone listens to them. Why does everyone give importance to their opinion? Why do people trust them? And how do they get people to follow them, so much so that people are willing to do go out of their way for them? If you really want to learn how leaders create this charisma, then the next chapter is extremely critical.

Chapter Summary

▶ Stop blaming and complaining.

▶ Take 100% responsibility for your life and every situation – positive or negative.

▶ Use the Responsibility Formula – Situations + Response = Results (S+R=Re).

▶ If you change your response, you can change your situation and results.

▶ How you respond will determine what kind of results you get.

▶ Taking responsibility is one way to gain power, while blaming and complaining results in the loss of power, energy and time.

▶ Ask yourself Responsibility Questions rather than blame and complain questions.

4

Charismatic Leadership

Leaders have charisma which attracts people to them. The charisma of a leader is obvious when you see people following them wherever they go. I am sure you have heard about managers who are followed by their subordinates to the new organizations they join. This happens when people have so much faith in the professional integrity and leadership of those individuals. This chapter is all about discovering how leaders create that charisma to create such following.

Have you ever wondered, why is it that when companies like Reliance, Tata or Birla declare that they are starting a new business, thousands of people want to invest in their new business ventures? Why do people follow these business leaders so blindly? What makes them so charismatic?

Charismatic leaders can be found in any industry, not necessarily just in business. For example, when a leading Indian actor like Amir Khan announces his upcoming film, everyone wants to go and see it. People are also confident that the film would provide entertainment of a superior quality. Even though there is a possibility of it not meeting expectations and being a flop, people still flock to the cinema hall to watch the film on the very first day. Why? Why do people blindly follow actors like Amir Khan? What makes them so charismatic?

The answer to this question is actually quite simple. *The charisma of a leader comes from the consistent results he creates.* The reason we blindly follow leaders in any industry, is because they create consistent results.

For instance, we know that most business ventures started by Reliance, Tata and Birla have mostly been successful in the past. We know that movies starring actors like Amir Khan, Amitabh Bachchan and Salman Khan have mostly been successful and entertaining in the past. Looking at the consistency of their results, we are willing to trust them and follow them. So while there could be others reasons for a leader's charisma, like money, fame, power, looks and the like, the real reason for their charisma is actually the fact that they deliver consistent results.

To explore this line of thought, let us think – why have people stopped following stars like Vinod Khanna and Dharmendra? How come they have lost their charisma? The answer is quite obvious; it's because they were not consistent with creating the kinds of results they used to. Now some people would say it's because they are old.

Well in that case, why do people still follow Amitabh Bachchan who is also as old? Again, the answer lies in the fact that Bachchan still delivers super hit movies. In fact he keeps experimenting and betters the quality of his films in terms of film choices as well as performances. The fact is, the day he would start doing mediocre films consistently, people would stop following him, as he would lose his charisma without the consistent hits.

The same principle applies to business leaders like Reliance. If they start making consistent losses for their investors, eventually they would lose their charisma and people would stop investing in their stocks. But the moment they show consistent results, they would regain their charisma and their stock value would increase again. So the bottom line is:

Consistent results – create charisma

Do we all get attracted to people who deliver results consistently? Naturally you will get attracted to people who create consistent results. Will you give them more value? Will you listen to them? I am sure you definitely will!

All of us want to listen to people who have something meaningful to share; people who we believe have achieved something, rather than those who have not really made a difference. It is the people who create results consistently who exude some sort of charisma, owing to their constant and consistent success. Their success draws people towards them magnetically.

It isn't so much to do with their personality or individual charm, as much it has to do with consistent performance and success. This phenomenon is not limited to people alone; companies like flipkart.com or makemytrip.com are ideal examples of how their consistent results have ensured that they have a huge following in the market.

The real puzzle however is, how is it that leaders have the ability to create consistent results? Are they lucky? Do they have better resources? What is the secret to their repeated success?

The answer to this question is really simple, but not at all easy. The strongest quality of a leader is the weakest quality of a person with the employee mindset. The reason leaders are able to create consistent results is because they have the power of commitment and zero tolerance for excuses.

The Power of commitment and zero tolerance for excuses

The concept of commitment is one that was actually quite strong in the Indian culture: the power of the word, or *zubaan*. A popular saying in Hindi/Urdu goes: *Ek baar zabaan de di, to phir jaan jaye par zabaan na jaye*; which means. Once a promise is made, or word is given, then one's life can be lost but the promise cannot be broken.

This sense of commitment however, is on the decline these days. Thus it has become even more precious and a hallmark of leaders.

Leaders stick to their commitments and also have zero tolerance for excuses. They do not tolerate excuses from anyone, including themselves. Their level of commitment is such that they are usually more than willing to go through any amount of discomfort to create their results.

On the other hand, ordinary people with the employee mindset always have more excuses than results. When excuses outweigh results, others gradually realize that such people cannot be trusted. This leads to such people being valued lesser as time goes by.

So when a leader says that he will call you in the evening at 5 o'clock, with some work done, you can be sure to get that phone call with the positive news or if the work is not done for some reason, he will definitely call to communicate the status and provide a fresh deadline.

I am sure you have known such people in your life as well. And it is for such people that you surely have a lot of respect and regard, for their ability to keep their commitments consistently.

On the other hand, if someone with an employee mindset tells you that he will call you in the evening at 5 o'clock with some work done, you know that most probably their work will not be done. They may not even bother to inform you about the delay. You know you cannot rely on these people because they always have some excuse or the other for not getting things done. In fact you will find that there are many people around who don't keep their commitments and keep making excuses. Those who keep their commitments are actually rare.

It is this lack of valuing commitments that is actually also coming in the way of India's growth to becoming a world leader. A nation is the sum of her people – if the people do not value their commitments and keep their word, not much progress can be made by the nation as a whole. This may be uncomfortable, but it is the truth of our country and it is time to deal with it and change it. There are many examples of this around us in our day to day life some of which are –

- If you call a plumber to get some work done, you are doubtful whether he will come on time. Even when he comes late, he never apologizes for being late. He may make some excuse for being late and think that it is justified.
- If a key member of your team is supposed to complete something on a particular date, chances are that he may not finish it. Rather he has excuses ready and feels that he is justified for not completing the work on time.
- When a person commits to his family to be home on time, his family knows that he may be late. When he reaches late he has excuses that he thinks are justified.
- A common man promises to follow traffic rules when he gets a driver's license. But most people break traffic rules like overtaking from the wrong side, not stopping at the traffic signal and the like.
- Invariably people reach late for meetings, dinner invitations, conferences, and other events.

There are endless examples of how most people are ordinary people with the employee mindset, who give more excuses than results. There are very few people in organizations who are leaders with the entrepreneur mindset who keep their commitments. And for some reason if they are not able to keep their commitments, they will definitely communicate, apologize with humbleness and give another commitment which they will surely keep.

With the world becoming an increasingly complex place, the need for leaders keeps growing. The kind of leaders required, are people who can keep their commitments. Imagine, a world full of such committed leaders, who keep their commitments no matter what, be it personal or professional. The world would become an even better place to live in. To be a part of this exciting and promising reality, the first step is to change ourselves. By doing so, we take the first step towards changing the world.

Become a charismatic leader by keeping your commitments

- Reach on time for meetings.
- Communicate and apologize for any delays.
- Go out of your way to keep your commitments for project deadlines.

- Don't make excuses; instead ask for support if you need something to maintain your commitments.
- When you tell someone you will email them, make sure you email them on time.
- When you tell someone you will call them, make sure you call them on time.
- When you tell your boss you will finish something, make sure you finish it.

When Ratan Tata declared that he would make a car for only Rs. one lakh, he ensured that he kept his commitment. This meant that he would probably make less profit that way, but for him his word to the public and his commitment to the masses was more important than profit.

When commitments are maintained against all odds, the charisma of the person increases exponentially!

Commitment begins at home

- Reach home on time when you have promised you would.
- Communicate and apologize for delays.
- Go out of your way to keep your commitments of holiday plans.
- Give quality time to your family, not just excuses.
- When you promise your child a chocolate, make sure you give him a chocolate, not excuses!

I ensure that I have a great family life by keeping all my promises made to my family. I am extremely committed to having a great family life and a great marriage with my wonderful life partner, Indu.

Be a charismatic leader in your country by being a great citizen

- Follow the traffic rules.
- Don't bribe people and spoil your own country's system.
- Pay your taxes on time.
- Demand high commitments from people.
- Do some charity work; don't just make excuses for the way things are.
- Keep your commitment of being a great citizen in whatever way you can.

Steve Jobs was extremely sensitive to delivering his commitments with excellence, in design as well as quality. That is why Apple Computers has such a huge fan base – because Steve Jobs always delivered his commitments and gave the market stunning design and quality.

Steve Jobs believed: 'Design is not just what it looks like and feels like, design is also how it works'. He had zero tolerance for excuses and would accept nothing less than excellence from his team.

Charisma is not something people are born with. It is a quality that you get attributed with, once you start producing consistent results, maintaining commitments and having zero tolerance for excuses. Here are some simple guidelines to help you keep commitments:

1. **Think before you commit** – Make sure you take a moment to think before you commit, before you give your *zubaan*. Ask yourself, if you are sure you will be able to honour the commitment you

are making. Only once you are confident that you can, make the commitment. The biggest reason for people not being able to keep their commitments is because they make it without giving it enough thought. Most people are in the habit of over-promising and under-delivering. And this is something that all of us have done in our lives. The point is to not feel bad about what is already gone by, but decide to never make a commitment before first giving it adequate thought.

2. **Use mobile reminders** – The one thing which is our constant companion these days is the cell phone. Remember, your cell phone besides being your constant companion is quite well-equipped to function as a personal secretary, if one is able to use its functions well.

   Whenever you make a commitment – big or small, make sure you immediately create a reminder in your mobile calendar, so that you can make sure that you remember commitments. Don't use the to-do feature; create a calendar reminder so that you can see how your day is scheduled when you make commitments. Starting today make sure you start using your mobile reminders, because with the amount of work and information that you are handling, it is almost impossible to remember everything without some support system. Make your mobile your best support system, starting today.

3. **Apologize for your mistakes without making excuses** – No one is perfect and we all make mistakes. Whenever you make the mistake of not keeping your commitments, make sure you apologize instantly without making excuses. The moment you make an excuse, your mind learns that it is justified to not keep your commitments. The way to have zero tolerance for excuses is not to give any excuses. Learn to say: 'I am sorry this shouldn't have happened.' And add: 'This will not happen again'. When you apologize without any excuses you feel truly sorry, and thus

it helps you to keep your commitments the next time. It is easy for people also to give you another chance when you apologize without making any excuses.

4. **Practice making definite commitments** – The only way to become a master at something is to practice it again and again. The issue is, most people in our country don't want to practice making commitments. If you ask people by when they can expect a call, they say: 'May be sometime next week' In fact some people even say: 'I can't promise exactly when, but maybe sometime next week'. The reason most people don't want to commit, and the reason they use the word 'maybe' is so that no one can hold them accountable. But this way, people keep getting worse at keeping commitments. So start building the muscle of your commitment power, by regularly making definite commitments, and not saying 'maybe'. Practice giving a specific time and date; make it specific, make it a strong commitment and become accountable for it. The more you practice it, the better you get at it. If you fail, apologize and make a fresh commitment, simple.

5. **Communicate before time** – I have realized that the biggest reason for most customers getting angry is not because people delay doing things on time; it's because people don't communicate before time for delays. Most customers are reasonable people and are willing to understand the amount of work pressure that we all face nowadays. But what customers can't understand is, why people can't make a simple phone call to communicate before time and set clear expectations about a new timeline. Not only with customers, but in every area of life you will see people getting angry for this reason. When the husband does not reach home on time, the wife is angry not because he came late, but because he did not care to even call and communicate. Stop taking people for granted; stop making excuses, and make that phone call before time to communicate and let people know that you need a new deadline. Yes, you might have

to negotiate or handle their anger, but that is better than losing their trust completely. Moreover, if you keep your commitments most of the time, then people will mostly trust your reasons when you communicate before time, instead of doubting you. So make sure you get into the habit of communicating before time.

6. **Demand commitment from people and inspire leadership** – The reason I have become a leader in my line of work is because my mentors always demanded commitments from me and had zero tolerance for excuses. In fact the only way to be fair with someone is to expect the best from them. Expect people to keep their commitments with you, tell them that their excuses are not ok! Encourage them to be leaders. It is one thing to practice leadership, and another to inspire leadership in others. In fact it will become extremely easy for you to keep your commitments when people in your environment start keeping their commitments. So start demanding commitments and have zero tolerance for excuses.

7. **Stop being a liar and have the courage to be honest** – Most people in the world are liars. Even when they have not finished their work on time or with the expected quality, they still say: 'Yes it's done'. The most dangerous part is when people become comfortable with lying. Being a liar kills one's self-esteem and makes one live in constant fear. So make sure you stop lying; if you make a mistake be honest about it and be brave enough to face the consequences. If you don't face the consequences of your false commitments, you will definitely continue making more false commitments. Be a leader and have the courage to be honest and tell the truth, practice saying: 'I have not finished it yet' or 'I forgot to do it because I was casual about it'. The best way to become powerful is to be honest. Starting today, make sure you practice the courage to be honest in the most difficult of times, because your self-esteem and your inner power are more important than any consequences of your mistakes.

Here is an extremely important exercise to help you keep your commitments. Start with recognizing what are the excuses you make in different areas of your life and decide to have zero tolerance for these excuses. Use the following table to know yourself better:

Excuses I make for not having great health	Excuses I make for not having great relationships in my family	Excuses I make for not having great relationships at office	Excuses I make for not making progress in my career

Be brutally honest with yourself while filling in this table and feel free to add any more columns if you need to. The idea is to start confronting every single excuse that you make to yourself and to people around you so that, you can be sure you have zero tolerance for them, starting now.

If you sincerely practice and master keeping your commitments and stop making excuses, I promise you, only in a few days you will have such magnetic charisma, that people will start noticing a positive aura around you. In a few months people will start paying more attention to what you say, because they would know there is value to your words. If you continue keeping your commitments, in a few years a time will come when you say something and it will definitely happen; because you said it would happen. In fact people would swear by your commitments! That can be the extent of your charisma.

If you think what I am saying is too simple to be true, then you can look up all the mythological gods – one of the main reasons for their charisma is their ability to keep their word. Once Shiva, Krishna, Sai Baba, Satyanarayan or any *bhagwan* gave his word, it was final and thus their word came to be known as *vardaan*.

People were also scared of them because once they said something to punish you, it was a curse. The bottom-line – their word was enough to be a *vardan* or a curse. If you continually practice the seven simple steps given above, soon your charisma would be god-like!

For just one week try keeping every small and big commitment that you make to anyone in your life. I invite you to challenge yourself, to follow the seven steps to be a charismatic leader by keeping your commitments with people in your organization, in your family and even in your country starting now.

In my workshops we make people do this exercise on the very first day. After the workshop we always get feedback that this was one of the most important leadership practices they learnt. As a result, people became more and more charismatic by creating extraordinary results in their organizations and even in their families.

In fact many times I have the top official's wife call me and thank me saying: "I don't know what you did to my husband, but ever since the time he has returned from the workshop, he has shown amazing commitment towards me and the children, which was missing earlier. Thank you so much".

Senior managers who had not gone for holidays for many years soon took their families on vacation. They basically decided to create a balance in their lives. Bosses called me thanking me because their teams had become more committed than ever before and their performances had sky-rocketed.

All this is possible for anyone who practices the leadership qualities described in this book. In the next chapter, we will learn about how leaders are able to maintain their productivity even in times of pressure. How they keep their cool even during conflicts; how they handle problems instead of getting affected by them, how leaders are more effective during crises, when ordinary people get into depression; how leaders don't get hurt by people or situations easily. Once you master the techniques described in the next chapter, you will have the power to stand strong in any situation of your life and deal with any kind of person effectively.

Chapter Summary

▶ Leaders have a magnetic charisma that gets them a huge following.

▶ Consistent results create charismatic leaders.

▶ Leaders create their results by keeping their word.

▶ Leaders have zero tolerance for excuses.

▶ Use the following strategies for keeping your commitments and have zero tolerance for excuses.

▶ Think before you commit.

▶ Use mobile reminders.

▶ Apologize without making excuses.

▶ Practise making definite commitments.

▶ Communicate before time.

▶ Demand commitment from people and inspire leadership.

▶ Stop being a liar and have the courage to be honest.

▶ Make a list of all the excuses you make in every area of your life and have zero tolerance for them.

▶ Take up the seven day challenge to follow all the seven steps and keep all your commitments.

5

Emotional Intelligence – Leadership During Crisis

When India was under British rule, many people were depressed about losing their right to freedom. People who were helpless and weak decided to join the British army for survival. Many people felt powerless, and thought they were ordinary people who could not do anything about political affairs.

However, during this time of crisis there were people who were feeling confident, strong and decided to revolt against the British government and demand freedom.

Amongst many others these were leaders like Gandhi, Bhagat Singh, Chandra Shekhar Azad and Nehru. Some of the great leaders who we owe our independence to while others were feeling scared, depressed, helpless and powerless, these leaders were feeling determined, confident, powerful, creative, calm and in control – very different response to the same situation. Ultimately, the way we feel creates our actions and our actions create our results.

What we feel creates action and these actions produce results

Unlike ordinary people, leaders have the ability to manage their emotions intelligently and so are able to produce results even in high pressure situations. They are able to keep their calm even in a crisis. This ability is known as Emotional Intelligence (EI) which is a MUST for anyone who wants to be a leader.

In today's world, the pressure we are facing personally and professionally, is so much that emotional intelligence has become a necessity for all of us. Most people however, are still focussed only on logical intelligence. Logical intelligence which is conventionally known as Intelligence Quotient (IQ) is necessary, but it is not enough to become a great leader. In fact leadership requires more of emotional intelligence than logical intelligence; the ability to manage oneself and others.

What is emotional intelligence?

Emotional intelligence is your ability to manage your emotions during difficult situations.

- How do you feel when things don't go your way?
- How do you feel when people don't behave the way you want?
- How do you feel when you don't get results for your efforts?

I am sure you agree that if you feel powerful, you can deal with any difficult situation efficiently. However, if you are not in control of your feelings then *you are not in control of situations.* Most people don't have much control of their emotions. If things don't go their way, they can't help but feel upset; if people don't behave as per their expectations they can't help but feel angry; if they don't get results for their efforts they can't help feeling de-motivated. In fact, many people proudly say that they are very emotional, but what they are really saying is that they have very little or no control over their emotions.

Feeling angry, sad, helpless, humiliated, anxious, irritated, upset, depressed and the like are all natural emotions. But when you can't help feeling them over and over again, then that is definitely a sign of emotional weakness. **Emotional intelligence is about having the power to manage your emotions by choice.** An emotionally intelligent person would rarely say: 'I can't help feeling sad, anger, upset' and so on.

Let me share with you a personal experience wherein I faced a business crisis and due to my awareness of emotional intelligence, I was able to convert a crisis situation into an opportunity:

Many years ago I was working with a network marketing company and was partnering with one of my best friends – Sultan. Most of our networking business was based in a small town called Aurangabad where Sultan lived. In around six months we had about 500 people who had joined our network and our business was doing exceedingly well. All of a sudden, the organisation we were working for, decided to shut down their operations. Overnight we lost everything we had worked for in the last six months. There were 500 people who had joined our network and we were responsible for their investments too.

People were enraged and wanted a return of their investments. However, the company had shut down and was not willing to return any funds. Our initial response was tension, fear and panic, and then we decided to convert this crisis into an opportunity.

Our first step was to control and eliminate the negative emotions of fear and panic for ourselves and the team. We then consciously decided to remain strong emotionally, to be confident in the belief that we can control the situation. Once our emotions were in control, it helped us to be more creative and we were able to think of many different ideas to deal with the crisis.

We held a meeting for the entire network and decided to focus on converting their anger into courage and understanding. When everyone arrived, they were angry and upset about the loss of their investments. We heard them out patiently but did not allow their anger to get us upset or angry. Once people had finished what they wanted to say, for about 15 minutes I confidently spoke to people about being inspired rather than de-motivated, being powerful rather than weak, in order to deal with this crisis. Then Sultan spoke for about 30 minutes to inspire people and help them manage their emotions first. In only 45 minutes we had the entire crowd of 500 people calm down. Their anger had now subsided and they were feeling hopeful and courageous and ready to understand. Suddenly they saw this situation as an opportunity to become better leaders rather than remain in a state of anger. That was one of the best meetings we ever had. We won the trust of our team and together came out of the crisis like heroes. It was an experience that I can never forget!

This is how high emotional intelligence can help you create success even during a crisis situation. Today Sultan is a very successful trainer and real estate businessman. His clients are affluent people living abroad. He invests their funds and provides high financial returns in a short period of time. His success is no doubt due to his high emotional intelligence.

Here is another story that says a lot about emotional intelligence:

Business or professional crisis is one thing, and health crisis is another. One of my mentors – Dr. Sudhir Arora is one of the best behavioural trainers in India. For some reason, he had a health crisis which was completely unexpected. He was suffering from internal bleeding in his body along with extreme pain. He was advised emergency surgery to stop the bleeding. However doctors could not identify the root cause of the ailment.

A couple of days after the surgery he had internal bleeding from another part of his body and he had to go through a second surgery to control it. He seemed alright after the second surgery, but in a few days the bleeding recurred, and he had to go through a third surgery. Subsequently, he went through seven major surgeries and spent his life savings undergoing medical treatment. His health was very poor and he had constant stress and pain. This would have been the end of most men in his position.

But thanks to Dr. Arora's high emotional intelligence, he was in high spirits despite the pain he was undergoing. Emotionally he never let himself feel depressed, on the contrary he was always smiling and said that he felt blessed for all the support he was getting from his family and friends. He was physically weak and yet emotionally strong all the time. As a result he was able to bounce back to good health in a year's time and is currently inspiring thousands of people through his training programmes once again.

People with high EI (Emotional Intelligence) can deal with any situation powerfully, while people with low EI lose control of their life in the face of the smallest crisis.

When there is a recession and the market is down, how people and organizations respond emotionally, decides who the market leader is. While there are people who feel powerless emotionally – feeling worried and depressed during recession, there are others who feel emotionally powerful – creative, strong and inspired to convert recession into an opportunity. I am sure you have heard of people who became millionaires even during the recession; these people are leaders with an entrepreneur mindset.

During a financial crisis, there are people who feel restless, short tempered, irritated while dealing with family members and colleagues. While there are others who feel centred, calm, and inspire all those around them. They have the faith that their situation will definitely change for the better. This response is one of high emotional intelligence. The bottom line is, how you feel decides the quality of your life.

What is your emotional intelligence? How do you respond to a crisis, problem or conflict situation?

- How do you feel and respond in a situation of conflict with your boss?
- How do you feel and react when your wife does not agree with your decision?
- What do you feel on receiving negative feedback?
- What is your reaction when you find out that you have made a mistake?
- How do you feel when you are not able to meet your commitments?
- How do you tackle the feeling of failure?
- What is your reaction when your colleague is appreciated, instead of you?
- When someone breaks your trust – how do you respond emotionally? What do you feel?

Awareness of your emotional patterns

The above questions will help you identify your emotional patterns, which will in turn enable you to develop your emotional intelligence. Emotional patterns are the emotions that usually surface as a course of habit in response to various situations.

For example, when a boss gives negative feedback to a team of three people, all of them respond differently, based on their emotional patterns. One of the team members may feel angry, the other may feel sad, and the third may feel motivated to work better. Each one of them reacts on the basis of their emotional patterns. Thus, the same situation triggers a different reaction for each individual.

Haven't you had an experience when your father or mother's scolding motivated you, while it de-motivated your brother or sister? Haven't you had an experience when your friend was very angry about something while you felt pretty calm about the same thing? Different people feel differently in the same situation simply because of the difference in their emotional patterns. If you have a strong emotional pattern it is emotional intelligence, but if you have a weak emotional pattern it is emotional weakness.

To take my example, post marriage I found myself getting irritated at minor issues. This was an emotional pattern that emerged from being used to getting my own way. With time and practice I learnt to change this emotional pattern and stopped blaming my wife, Indu, for the discord.

A typical response to my wife getting upset would be my angry response with a desire to overwhelm and dominate. This issue is faced by many husbands and can be changed once we are aware of our emotional patterns. Let us now take a look at the emotional pattern of extraordinary leaders:

In South Africa, Nelson Mandela was fighting against the government by creating a militant army. As a result of this, he was arrested, convicted and sentenced to life imprisonment for attempt of violence against the government. Where ordinary people could lose their focus and feel completely lost, frustrated, angry and so on, Nelson Mandela chose to feel powerful, courageous, calm and inspired to win. This helped him to create powerful results in his life.

In 1990 he was released from prison, then in the year 1994 he was elected as President. He is one of the greatest leaders in the world whose emotional intelligence is difficult to match even today. Someone once asked him a question: 'How did you manage the suffering during the 26 years of imprisonment?' Nelson Mandela gave a confused expression and said: 'Who was suffering? I was preparing!'

It is emotional intelligence that gives leaders such as Nelson Mandela the ability to deal with crises and turn them into opportunities. But let's not stop at this, here is another inspiring story:

An 18 year old boy called Sunil Mittal had the dream of starting his own business. He borrowed Rs 20,000 as capital and started a business of manufacturing cycle spare parts in Ludhiana. However his dreams were bigger, and in order to achieve them he decided to shift his base to Delhi.

He started a new business of importing products from abroad and distributing them in local markets of India. During that time the Indian government made some new policies under which many imported products were banned. Unlike other business owners, Sunil Mittal did not feel disheartened. Instead he felt inspired and creative.

As a result he was able to spot opportunities, which probably *others could not.*

He was able to see that the telecom revolution was starting in India with the push-button technology. He grabbed at this opportunity to start manufacturing push-button telephones. He increased his business with cordless phones, answering machines, fax machines, and the like. A few years later the mobile phone arrived. But instead of feeling disheartened, he felt excited about this new technology. Seeking this new opportunity led him to start a mobile company called Airtel in 1995.

The rest as they say is history! Today Airtel is one of the biggest and most trusted mobile companies. Sunil Bharti Mittal has emerged as one of the most respected leaders of India and is recognized all over the world today. This would not have happened without his ability to look at the positive in everything – an outcome of his emotional intelligence.

It is possible for all of us to achieve great success in our own fields and even in our relationships, provided we develop our emotional intelligence by creating strong emotional patterns. The first step to achieve this is to become aware of our emotional patterns. Let us now engage in the following exercise which will help you to do so:

Emotional Pattern Awareness Exercise

Situations	Emotional Pattern (Feelings)	New Emotional Pattern (Feelings)
You don't get along with your boss		
Situation of conflict with your wife		
Someone gives you negative feedback		
When you make a mistake		
When things go wrong		

Above are some sample situations to get you started. However feel free to add your own situations from work place or family life, and jot down your current emotional patterns in those areas. This will help you to recognize how you usually react to certain situations and help you increase your awareness. Enhanced awareness will in turn enable you to make better choices in developing your emotional intelligence.

So if you habitually feel short-tempered during a conflict with your wife, you may choose your new emotional pattern of being understanding and humorous. If you habitually feel upset when your boss does not support you, then you can consciously choose new emotional patterns of feeling calm.

Remember that the quality of your emotions in any situation would create the quality of your actions and the quality of your actions would create the quality of your results. So if you want superior results in your life, start creating high emotional intelligence by becoming aware of your emotional patterns. Now consciously chose a new emotional pattern to feel differently in the same situation in order to improve your EI.

Post this exercise, people feel very excited about the change in their emotional patterns. However a common question people ask me is: 'How do I control what I feel?' Here are three powerful ways to control and change your emotional patterns:

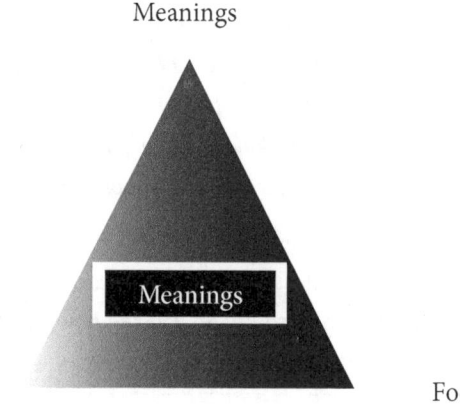

Controlling Emotions: Knowing How Emotions Work

The quality of our feelings is controlled by the quality of meanings we make. Feelings don't happen on their own. When a situation occurs, we first create a meaning about that situation and from that meaning, we get our emotions.

For example if you were asked to leave your organization due to layoffs, what meaning you make of this situation will control the way you feel in this situation. If the meanings you make are:

- *I am totally destroyed now that I have no job or*
- *How am I going to get a job fast enough to manage my monthly expenses? or*
- *It is useless being loyal to any company when they just don't care!*

You will obviously have negative feelings like anger, frustration, helplessness, worry, inferiority, depression and the like. But in the same situation if you make meanings like:

- *This is an opportunity for me to relook at the value I bring to my future organization.*
- *I always wanted to start a business of my own and this could be the opportunity I was waiting for.*
- *The company had no other choice. Besides job cuts sometimes benefit a lot of other employees.*
- *The company has done enough for me, now it's time to say goodbye and look for a better opportunity.*

With meanings like these, you will obviously have positive feelings like humility, gratitude, understanding, confidence, excitement to do something new and so on. So you see how you feel is controlled by the meanings you make in any situation.

During my workshops, some participants get a little angry and ask me, 'Am I not supposed to feel bad when I face injustice?' My answer is simple.

You can feel bad if you choose to or you can choose a totally different reaction. What you feel is your choice. Just be aware that your feelings will create your actions and your actions will create your results. It is pretty obvious that positive results come from positive actions, which come from positive feelings, which come from positive meanings to start with. A situation on its own does not have any meaning, it depends on what meaning we assign to it.

The Vital Chain: It Begins with a Meaning and ends with Results

There is no meaning in situations, except the meaning we choose to give them.

A simple formula to understand this is S + M = E which means Situations + Meanings = Emotions

Some people believe that leaders have great confidence during crises because they are born with this confidence and strength. We know that's not true! We are all born with a blank mind, which is conditioned as we grow up in an environment consisting of our family, friends, school teachers, society, media and so on. Our environment, our culture, our up-bringing have a great impact on the way we think and what meanings we create for situations in our lives. But that does not mean that situations are born with meanings, or that we are born with meanings. Here is a wonderful story to understand this better:

When you live in a country where African people are still looked down on just because of the colour of their skin, it is easy to get carried away by meanings like: 'A black man can never be the president of a country like America'. With such meanings one would obviously never be motivated to run for the presidential election. But one man dared to break this mass hypnotic meaning and decided to create his own meaning.

He probably believed in a meaning like: 'Everything is possible, if I believe in my dream. For something that has never happened before, there's always a first time'. With meanings like these I am sure, Barrack Obama was filled with a strong sense of confidence that he can fulfil his dream and be the first one to bring a change in America which would be exemplary for the whole world.

Just imagine the emotional experience Barack Obama would have gone through in the many years of his political career, where thousands of people must have told him that it was impossible for an African man to become President of America. But then as a leader he did not get carried away by the meanings people had created in their minds. He chose to create his own meanings. Like all great leaders he knew that any situation is what we choose to make of it. He understood the power of meanings and so had control over his feelings which has made him the most powerful man in the world today.

If you truly want to make your ambitions come to life, if you truly want your dreams to come true, then you must develop the leadership ability to choose the meanings you give to any situation and consequently choose your feelings, actions and results.

In my own case, I can say I have fulfilled my own dreams by creating high emotional intelligence by taking control of my meanings.

When I was in school I wasn't very good at studies, the meaning that my teachers made out of this was that I would never do very well in my life since I was not good at academics. Luckily I refused to believe in that meaning and the meaning I chose to make was: 'Success comes from smart work and experience, not necessarily from books and education'.

I started my career with a door-to-door sales job. That was the best job I ever had, in spite of facing a lot of rejections. It was my team leader, who kept motivating me on how I must turn every 'no' into a 'yes' rather than feeling de-motivated about it. My team leader explained that the value of one sale was ₹500.

He asked me to consider, that I had to go through about 20 customers before I got a 'yes' from a customer who would buy the product. In this case, he said that each 'no' was worth 500/20 = 25. He added that since it took me 20 'nos' to get to one 'yes', then each of them had a value of ₹25.

Now if you have one 'yes' worth ₹25, and 20 'nos' worth 25 then what is more valuable? Well logically I said 20 nos collectively are more valuable. My team leader said in that case I must have gratitude and excitement after every 'no', since it was giving me a value of ₹25 which I could collect from the last person who said 'yes' to me! That made a lot of sense to me and that month onwards I was always the champion in my sales team. Because every 'no' meant I got a valuable transaction worth ₹25, it made me more motivated and so I approached every new customer with more excitement than the one before.

This training taught me that failures never take us backwards; they always add value to our life to help us grow.

In the five years of my sales career, I grew from a Sales Executive to a Sales Manager where I had the opportunity to motivate and inspire my sales team. This is where I realized my strength as a trainer and how good I was at inspiring and motivating people. So I decided to become a behavioural trainer. At that time in India, there was hardly any scope for trainers. Many people told me, I was wasting my time, should take up a reasonable job and stop living in a dream world. But the meaning in my head was: 'I must look for opportunities or I must create my own opportunities.' With this meaning, I continued working as a freelance trainer doing small-time training programs.

Along the way I learnt from the best trainers in the world, by attending their workshops and learning cutting-edge technology in behavioral science. It became my passion to make transformational changes in organizations in record-breaking time. Since then, I have never looked back and I can say that today I am living all my dreams. In the last few years, I have had the privilege of training thousands of people in the corporate world and establishing myself as one of the most successful trainers in the country. I have worked with some of the best CEOs and top executives in the country and have had the privilege to both learn and work with them as their executive coach.

Another big leap in my career was when I learnt to fire-walk, and decided to use it in my corporate leadership workshops. Again, there were people who said it was too risky and not practical to do such a dangerous activity in corporate workshops. But the meaning that I drew was: 'Everything is possible if you do it the right way' I also had another meaning: 'Anything done with precision and perfection can create results, not accidents.' With such great meanings, I took another leap of faith with confidence and became one of the pioneers of introducing fire-walking in India. As a result, I have been able to create mind-blowing results for people in two-hour workshops, where people learn to face their fears by walking on fire.

The biggest fire-walk event I conducted was with 2,400 people over a span of four days which helped them to create a sales turnover of ₹250 crores. More than 10,000 people have walked with me on fire and experienced their true potential by learning to change the meanings they give to situations like walking on fire.

It is due to emotional intelligence that I have achieved all my dreams, and if I can do it, so can you.

As leaders it is important that you master the art of making powerful meanings, so that you can inspire others around you as well; just like my team leader had inspired me by giving powerful meanings about 'nos'.

Remember the quality of your meanings will create the quality of your emotions or feelings, which will create your actions and results.

The Secret to Results: Your Emotions

Are you ready then? Because now it's your turn to walk on fire with me, by doing the following exercise and improve your emotional intelligence.

Let's exercise your meaning-making muscles to make positive meanings for the following situations:

- My team member does not listen to me

_____

_____

_____

_____

- I don't have the money to start my own business

_____

_____

_____

_____

- I did not get the appraisal I was expecting this year

_____

_____

_____

_____

_____

- My wife does not express her love the way I want her to

_____

_____

_____

_____

_____

- My children don't listen to me

_____

_____

_____

_____

_____

Once you are done with the above, here's another exercise for you. Write down situations from your personal and work life wherein an improvement is required on your emotional intelligence front and then note down the meanings you think you need to change.

Let us learn the second way to improve our emotional intelligence.

Physiology controls emotions

I read a beautiful story once about how God wants us to find our unlimited power, but he also wants only the worthy ones to find it; only the ones who were truly willing to work for it. So he thought about where he would hide the power, so that only those who truly work for it, would find it. God thought a lot, and then he decided to put our unlimited power in the place where we would never look for it.

He hid it in our bodies, because he knew that working on one's body was the hardest thing for a human being. But those who do work on their bodies will definitely find the treasure of unlimited power, the power to control their emotions and even influence other people's emotions.

When I heard of this story for the first time I was quite sceptical, but then I learnt the scientific aspects of how our physiology – our body has a huge impact on our emotions. In this chapter I am going to share the facts I learnt about how this works, because I discovered that we have unlimited power in our bodies to control our emotions and even to influence other people's emotions.

Improve your EI through your physiology from within yourself, because your *physiology controls your emotions!*

You are probably wondering, what is physiology? Physiology is the way your body reacts when you are in a certain emotional state. You may also call it body language, but for now we will stick to the word physiology.

In fact it has now been scientifically proven, that our mind and body are not separate, they are fully integrated. Here is a question to start you off on understanding the mind-body integration.

When you feel low in energy, does it impact your physiology i.e. your body language? I am sure your answer is yes. And not just you, everyone in the world will agree that when they feel low or high, it immediately shows up in their physiology. So if you are happy and high in energy it is obvious that it will impact your physiology immediately. If a person feels confident it shows up in their physiology, if the same person is feeling insecure, that too shows up in their physiology.

Whether you feel low or high in energy, positive or negative, it always impacts your physiology. What this proves is that *your emotions and your physiology cannot go in two different directions.*

The Strong Link between Physiology and Emotions needs to be understood

For example, if I ask you to adopt the following body language:

- shoulders completely loose
- head down with a sulky face
- breath shallow and slow.

Now if I ask you to feel excited, is it possible? No it won't be possible for you to feel excited because your physiology would not support the emotion of excitement. Let's try it right now! I would really like you to engage with this concept and realize it, rather than just understand it theoretically.

So you would need to stand up and keep your shoulders completely loose; put your head down facing the floor and make a sulky face. Then make your best effort to feel excited.

I promise you, you won't succeed because your physiology just won't allow you. Don't just believe me blindly, try it yourself right now before you read any further.

I bet you were not able to feel excited because technically, it is just not possible for your emotions and physiology to go in two different directions. Your physiology and emotions always go hand in hand.

But you already knew this didn't you! Well here is a breakthrough understanding in the science of physiology which most people are not aware of.

If our physiology is controlled by our emotions then our emotions can also be controlled by our physiology!

What this means is that if you consciously change your physiology, you can use it to make yourself feel high or powerful in any situation at any given time, almost instantly. All extraordinary leaders understand this and thus whenever they face difficult situations, the first thing they control is their physiology and thus they take control of their emotions.

| Take control of Physiology | ⇨ | Take control of Emotions |

The Symbiotic Relationship between Physiology and Emotions

Now this may be too simple to believe but here are some references of great leaders who take control of their emotions by taking control of their physiology.

Whenever Sachin Tendulkar faces a difficult situation in cricket, he does not get into a negative physiology, rather he consciously gets into a more powerful physiology, which helps him to be in a positive state of mind. The best sportsmen in the world, condition themselves to be in a state of great physiology even in the most difficult times. Does this mean that Sachin Tendulkar always wins when he is in a great state of physiology? No, not necessarily and not always. But do you think it helps him to be in a positive emotional state to have a possibility of winning? Yes, absolutely. Having a positive physiology will definitely help anyone to stay in positive emotional state, which obviously increases your chances for positive results.

On the contrary imagine Sachin using negative physiology while reacting to a negative situation in the game, do you think that would help him to win the game? Absolutely not!

But consciously choosing a positive body state is not always practically possible, because once you are in a low state there is very little awareness. In a low state, our emotions have total control of our body and thus we lose all control and get carried away. So what's the solution then?

The solution is to condition your physiology to be in a high and positive state all the time so that you are ready when you face difficult situations. For example, sports champions like Sachin Tendulkar, Tiger Woods and others train in advance to condition their physiology and remain in a high positive state at all times. So during their practice sessions they deliberately smile, keep their chest high, keep their shoulders strong and use a confident body language. When they do this again and again, their body gets conditioned into a positive state and hence whether their game is going well or not, you don't see their confidence going down because their physiology supports them to continue feeling strong and confident.

Here is another simple example to understand this. Think of a person in your office or in your work environment whom you look up to as a leader. Now think about how their physiology is at the beginning of the day, as well as at the end of the day. I bet you will realize that this person remains in a positive emotional state because their physiology is in a high positive state at all times, including at the end of the day.

Most other people in the office lose energy by the end of the day, because they have a very loose physiology by the end of the day. How come extraordinary people have more energy at the end of the day? Because when they condition themselves to be in a high positive physiology at all times they literally generate high energy from within themselves at any time of the day. Thus leaders are actually energy generators!

Here is how I applied this strategy to generate high energy while writing this book. I always do my writing work at night, when there is no one to disturb me. However, the disadvantage of that is that by the end of the day, many times I would feel tired and not have the energy to write. But I know that all of us have unlimited energy within us, which we can access by using our physiology correctly.

So to manage my emotions what I did was to stand straight with shoulders high like a soldier at attention. I would salute and say: *'Jai hind'* with a lot of power, and then I would make a fist and say 'Yes!' three times. By doing this exercise, I was consciously generating high energy from within myself. I would repeat this for two or three minutes, and amazingly I was able to feel strong, full of energy and then I would sit and write in a positive state of mind.

Notice yourself in the office when you sit with negative physiology; what happens to your energy levels when you sit in the chair, with your back slouched and shallow breathing? You start feeling lazy and sleepy even at the beginning of the day sometimes, don't you? Now what if you consciously sit with a more upright posture and maintain a gentle smile on your face? Do you think it would help you feel energetic and more positive towards your work? I bet it will!

That is why when you go for Yoga, the first thing you learn is to maintain the right posture to create balance. If you go to learn martial arts, the first thing you learn is the right posture to create strength. If you go for meditation, the first thing you learn is to maintain the right posture to create a sense of peace and calm. If you join the armed forces, the first thing you learn there is also to maintain a powerful and strong body language at all times. No wonder soldiers have more emotional strength compared to civilians!

The best of soldiers, sportsmen, spiritual gurus, yoga masters and martial arts experts are people who focus on conditioning their body to a very high and positive physiology, because they realize that the only way to manage results is to manage emotions and the way to manage our emotions is to condition our physiology.

Here is a superb experiment done to prove how our physiology can completely change our emotional states. In a hospital where a lot of patients were being treated for depression and trauma, they chose the ten most depressed patients and assigned one security guard to each one of them. They were taken off all medicines and were prescribed to keep a gentle but consistent smile on their faces throughout the day without any reason. The security guards were ordered to make sure that their patients kept smiling consistently.

This was done for a month and after that it was a miracle to observe, that all these ten patients had no signs of depression, as their emotions were now controlled by the new physiology which had been conditioned by smiling. As a result, all these patients were able to overcome depression and thus regain control over themselves.

With experiments like these, behavioral scientists realized that how we use our physiology can create certain chemical responses in our brains, which in turn creates certain emotions in us. But I believe this experiment had succeeded years ago in the movie industry.

Did you know that many actors like Amitabh Bachchan, Shahrukh Khan, Amir Khan, actually end up crying in a lot of emotional scenes while shooting even though they are acting? This just proves their versatility, they are so involved in playing the character that they actually get into the emotional state of sadness in reality. That is why their acting seems so realistic, because they have the ability to get into character through their physiology.

Bad actors are those who don't get into character completely, as they don't know how to get into the exact physiology of their character. As a result when they cry or laugh it does not seem realistic. You can clearly tell that the person is acting. In case of good actors we just don't feel they are acting, since they are so realistically involved in the character.

This is why actors like Amitabh, Shahrukh, Amir Khan and some others, lead the industry even today, because they have total control over their emotions and are able to use their physiology to control other  people's emotions too. You can actually make people feel anything you want, provided you have mastery over your feelings by achieving the requisite physiology.

So now it's your chance to be a leader and take control of your emotional intelligence. Starting now, sit straight and condition yourself to practice being in a positive and strong physiology.

Whenever you face a difficult situation, consciously get into a positive physiology and I guarantee, you will get the energy to deal with any situation.

Here is an exercise that I do during my workshops, which will help you also, to condition your physiology positively. I ask my participants to write down the answers to these questions:

- What are the situations in which you usually lose control over your emotions?
- What is the physiology you usually use in those situations?

- What new physiology would you now use to generate high emotional energy in the same situations?

Here is an example of a very senior manager who was doing this exercise:

Situations where you need high/positive energy?	What physiology do you usually use here?	What new physiology will you use to generate high energy?
After lunch	Slouching in my chair, hardly smiling	Sit straight in my chair, smile and take deep breaths
End of the day	Shoulders and body loose, a tired look on my face	Strong shoulders, upright body language, and a happy expression
When I have to stay extra hours at work	Make a dull face and work with negative physiology	Have a peaceful expression and work with a more positive physiology
When my boss is angry	Stern face, rude tone and high pitched voice	Calm face, light tone and assertive voice
When I reach home late and family is upset	Defensive physiology, angry face, raised voice	Accepting my mistake, apologetic face and loving voice

You can generate more energy to deal with any situation in your life, by simply taking control of your physiology. Do the above exercise right now and choose at least five situations where you can condition your physiology to be in a state of positive energy.

Since this is a scientific yet simple strategy, people find it very easy to implement and master it for generating energy and increasing their emotional intelligence. Imagine when you are constantly generating positive energy, people would love to be around you, would love to work with you, would be willing to come and resolve a conflict with you; they would be inspired by the positive energy you create in their environment. As a result of this, you will increase your following and become a leader who is a role model for many people.

Yet another way to improve your EI is Focus

Focus controls emotions

What is focus? **Focus refers to your thoughts and imagination.** When you feel something, it is always a result of what are you focusing on through your thoughts and images. For example, if a son is not home by the usual time and the mother feels worried, then for her to feel worried she must be focusing on thoughts and images that help her to feel worried. She could be thinking: 'I hope my son does not run into any trouble. Why is he so late? He is normally never so late. I hope everything is ok!' And she could be imagining her son having an accident, or him stuck in heavy rain and getting wet or having a fight with someone.

It is her thoughts and images that make her worried while on the other hand, the father is not worried at all. On the contrary, he is feeling quite confident that his son is alright because his focus is completely different and his emotions are completely different.

For the father to feel confident, he has to be focused on thoughts and mental images that help him feel confident. He could be thinking: 'My son is grown up now and he can take care of himself. He must be having fun with his friends. Or he must be stuck in traffic'. Along with these thoughts, he could be imagining his son as a strong and grown up man, or he could be imagining his son laughing and playing with his friends or his son driving and waiting in traffic. It is these thoughts and images that help the father to feel confident.

It is impossible to feel any emotion without focus i.e. without thoughts and imagination. If you were to lose your memory and you forgot all about your marriage, would you still have the emotions of love for your spouse? No you wouldn't, because the thoughts and images which helped you feel love for your spouse are lost. Do you agree? So you see, you can't manage your emotions if you can't manage your thoughts and mental images.

If emotion is like food, then thoughts and images are its ingredients. You can use thoughts and images in the right combination to create a recipe of any kind of emotion. The recipe of a spicy dish is very different from the recipe of a tangy dish. Similarly the recipe of anger is very different from the recipe of confidence. Every emotion requires the perfect recipe of specific types of thoughts and images which makes it the perfect emotion.

If the customer gives you feedback and you think: 'Why does he keep looking at the negative aspects of the product?' And then you imagine your customer to be a rude person with mean facial expressions. With this recipe, it is natural to feel negatively about customer feedback. However, you can also feel positive about the feedback by changing the recipe through your mental thoughts and images. Instead if you think – 'This customer is giving feedback because he expects high standards from us and is helping us with his feedback', and then imagine his helpful and smiling face, this recipe of thoughts and images will obviously make you feel positive about customer feedback.

Leaders like Narayan Murthy, Bill Gates, Sunil Mittal, Azim Premji and many others have high emotional intelligence because they control how they focus on most situations of their lives. They consciously create thoughts and images in their mind which help them have an empowering emotional response to any situation, rather than having a negative emotional response. Since they consciously control their focus most of the time, it becomes a habit for them to have positive emotional patterns instead of negative ones. But again you must condition your thoughts and images to focus in the right direction at all times, so that it becomes effortless for you to feel confident even during crises.

People in my workshops ask me whether it is possible to think and imagine positively even during negative situations or with negative people. And I say that the question is not: 'Can you change your emotions?' The question is: 'Do you want to change your emotions?' If you want to feel positive, then you must take conscious efforts to focus on positive thoughts and images and then you will feel positive even in negative situations or with negative people.

But I would repeat here, that if you have to consciously control focus during negative situations, then it would be difficult. So what you need to do is, condition your brain to focus on positive thoughts and images as a habit almost all the time. Only then will you be able to effortlessly manage your emotions in any situation and with any person.

When an organization goes through challenging times, the CEO must take control of what he is focusing on, because only then can he control his team's focus! People with an employee mindset have weak emotional patterns, because they focus on thinking negative and imagine the worst during a crisis and that's why they are followers. Leaders with the entrepreneur mindset lead the way by being the first to focus on positive thoughts and images during crisis and that is why they are leaders.

A great example is of a company who did this is Future Group in India, founded by another great leader called Kishore Biyani. Although he is very successful today, there was a time when he was failing in business over and over again.

Most people would have given up after so many failures but he pressed on. What differentiates leaders like him from others, is their high emotional intelligence. When others feel like giving up, people like Kishore Biyani feel even more determined to succeed.

When people like him fail they take control of their focus. Their prime thought is: 'How can I learn from my failure? How can I change my strategy to get what I want? How can I make sure I succeed next time? I am sure there is a way to succeed if I keep trying'. They also imagine themselves as successful in the future; they imagine themselves celebrating their success with their friends and family; they imagine the satisfaction of having done their best. With such powerful focus, it is possible for anyone to be a great leader like Kishore Biyani.

You can start becoming a leader by taking control of your focus right now, by doing the following exercise:

- Write down situations where you habitually experience negative emotions.
- Identify the thoughts and images behind those emotions.
- Consciously choose new thoughts and images which will create positive feelings.
- Now rehearse these new thoughts and images mentally again and again, to make them a habitual response.

The four steps mentioned above can help you to create high emotional intelligence by giving you conscious control over your focus. Remember focus controls feelings!

Do remember to email me your results. I would be happy to hear how you improved your Emotional Intelligence.

The next chapter will take your life to a completely new level. A level which you always wanted to reach! It is all about your personal vision as a leader.

Chapter Summary

▶ Unlike ordinary people, leaders have the ability to manage their emotions intelligently and hence are able to produce results even during pressure situations. They are able to keep their calm in crises.

▶ In today's world, the pressure we are facing personally and professionally is increasing so much that emotional intelligence has become a necessity for all of us.

▶ Emotional intelligence is your ability to manage your emotions during difficult situations.

▶ How you feel decides the quality of your life.

▶ You must learn to become aware of your emotional patterns if you want to develop your emotional intelligence.

▶ Emotional patterns mean your habitual emotions.

▶ Do the emotional awareness exercise to recognize your emotional patterns.

▶ There are three powerful ways of changing your emotional patterns:

• **Meanings control feelings:** The quality of our feelings is controlled by the quality of meanings we make. Feelings don't happen on their own. When a situation occurs, we first create a meaning about that situation and then comes the emotion.

• **Physiology controls emotions:** Physiology is the way your body reacts when you are in a certain emotional state. If you learn to change your physiology consciously, then you can learn to control your emotions.

• **Focus controls your emotions:** Focus comprises of your thoughts and imagination. When you feel something, it is always a result of what you are focusing on, through your thoughts and mental images. If you learn to consciously change your focus, you will learn to control your emotions.

6

Vision and Belief – The Most Critical Leadership Qualities

It goes without saying, that the most obvious and essential quality of a leader is to have a Vision. Leaders believe in their visions even when no one else believes in them. In most leadership books, this quality is given the highest priority and because of that it features pretty early as a chapter. The reason I talk about it much later in this book is because I believe that in order to be a leader, you must first train yourself to have high energy, high expectations, learn to take 100% responsibility, ensure commitment with zero tolerance for excuses and learn to have high emotional intelligence. Only after all of this, I believe, are we ready to create a vision and believe in it.

It is futile to have a vision without having the ability to work on it without the other qualities. I have met many people who have a vision, but have never achieved anything in their lives, simply because they lacked what it takes to fulfil their vision.

In your case, since you are ready with the first five pillars of leadership, you are ready to be an entrepreneur and move on to the next step of leadership by creating your own vision, instead of following the rest of the world.

Let's clarify, what is vision? People have different interpretations of this word, so let's explore what it means for leadership.

Vision is the ability to consciously create a goal and visualize that the goal is already achieved.

A person hires a taxi and tells the driver his destination. Half way through, he changes his mind and tells the taxi driver to take him to another destination. After a certain distance, he again changes his mind and directs the driver to another location. Fed up with his indecisiveness, the taxi driver stops the taxi and asks the guy to pay and leave. The taxi driver says: 'I am not interested in driving for someone who is not clear about where he wants to go.'

If even a taxi driver cannot help us without having a clear destination, then how can our destiny help us without a clear destination? Most people who work in organizations today, are not clear about their vision; they are working because they have a job to do. Even in businesses, people are just working because they have a business to handle. They go through the motions, without really knowing where they are headed.

The fact is that most people in the world don't have a clear vision, simply because they have not taken the effort to create one. People only have vague fancies, that they want a promotion, they want to be rich, happy, and successful, have a great relationship. But all these are goals with no specifications! A taxi driver cannot get you to your destination until he has the exact address for where you want to go. Similarly, life cannot help anyone who does not have a specific goal.

What stops people from creating and having a clear vision? The answer is simple – fear! Most people are afraid to create a clear vision because they fear failure. And thus they lose all chances of success. Leaders are successful because they have the courage to face failure.

A lot of people envy Bill Gates, but are unable to create a clear vision like him. He created a vision many years ago that he wants every computer in the world to use the Microsoft Operating System. That is why he is the leader of the IT industry today, but he went through many failures on the way.

Dhirubhai Ambani had a clear vision of creating India's biggest company and that is why Reliance is one of the biggest companies in the country today. That did not happen without encountering failures.

Ratan Tata had a vision of making the most economical car in the world and now we have the Tata Nano in our country. He too went through major failures before making it a success.

Shahrukh Khan had a vision of being the super star of India, which is what he is today. He too went through his share of failures in life.

Failure is not a barrier, it is a stepping stone to success. It is a signal that you are reaching closer to your destination. So have the heart to fail and start by creating a vision for yourself.

Success is not only chance, it is also a science. If success was only chance, most leaders would never be able to repeat their success. If you observe leaders, they succeed again and again because they know that success does not come by chance. Rather there is a method to it. Once you understand the science behind anything, you can repeat it and become successful repeatedly.

This method was used by a best selling author called Jack Canfield, who is the co-author of Chicken Soup for the Soul. His self-help books have sold over 100 million, copies and translated into more than 40 languages. But the fact is that his book was initially rejected by 140 publishers.

But leaders like him know that success is a science and hence can repeat it over and over again.

The most important part of the science of success is to first have a clear vision of your goal. Some simple steps to help you have a clear vision are:

1. **Create a vision which is clear and specific:** When you make a goal, be clear and precise. It's like ordering food in a restaurant. You cannot order saying, 'Get me the tastiest dish'. The waiter will still ask you for a specific order and you will have to state it clearly, so that he understands your order. Similarly, you must decide a clear vision for every area of your life whether it is physical, financial, career, relationships or spiritual. Make a clear and specific vision.

2. **Write the vision in visible places:** You must write your vision on paper and place it in visible places of your office and home both. This is important, as you should always have a clear view of your vision at all times.

3. **Believe in your vision, as if it has already been achieved through daily visualization:** The most important part of the vision is to believe that you have already achieved it. It is critical in the science of success to imagine daily that you have already achieved your vision.

4. **Take strategic action:** Make a strategy and start taking action. Never take action without strategy because you will waste time in making unnecessary mistakes. You always hear about top management having strategy meetings every year, because they know that every year they must strategize rather than acting blindly. Sometimes you may strategize only one step ahead and that's fine, but you must take strategic action.

Using these four simple steps, start creating your vision right away. Once you have the vision, believe in it!

You have probably heard of Roger Bannister, an athlete, who had the clear vision of becoming the best runner in the world by making a record of running one mile under four minutes. Many people told him that it was an impossible goal and even as per medical science in those days, it seemed impossible for the heart to sustain that kind of physical exertion.

But Roger believed in his vision and on May 6th 1954, he became the leader in his field by running one mile in 3 minutes and 54 seconds.

The best part was that within one year after that, 37 people followed the same science and broke his record.

What I learnt from this was that we must learn to believe in our vision, even when the whole world doubts it. It's just like how our parents believe in us even if the whole world doubts our capability; in fact they have faith in us even when we do not believe in ourselves. That's the kind of belief you must have in your vision.

Another amazing example is of a great actor called Jim Carrey, who had a clear vision of making $10 million as an actor. He even wrote a check to himself for $10 million, dating it for Thanksgiving Day 1995.

He kept this check in his wallet so he could always have visibility of his vision. As a result by 1995, after the great success of his movies like 'The Mask' his acting price went up to $20 million. When his father died, Jim placed the same check in his father's pocket as a tribute to him for helping nurture his dreams of becoming a star and for always believing in him.

Bruce Lee also followed the same steps towards success. He wrote down his goal in a letter to himself which is still displayed in a museum.

As a result of such a clear vision, it is not surprising that Bruce Lee achieved exactly what he wanted. To reiterate: success is a science;

you can achieve exactly what you want and the first step to that is
to create a clear vision.

Once you create a clear vision, you must also believe in it passionately. You see, the greatest leaders in the world were aware of the science of success and so knew that believing in their vision plays a big role in fulfilling it.

Scientific explanation of how beliefs play a big role in your results:

As human beings, we all have unlimited potential to achieve anything we want; but we are unable to take action towards our goals sometimes.

I am sure you have certain areas of your life where you want to take action and create extraordinary results, but you just don't feel motivated enough to take the required action. And that might make you feel that you don't have the required potential in that area. For example, you have a clear vision of losing ten kilograms of weight and you know exactly what you need to do for it. But you just don't feel motivated enough to take the action to lose that weight. Eventually you start feeling that you just don't have the potential or ability to lose weight.

Or you have a clear vision about making a certain amount of money and you even know how you can make it. But you just don't feel motivated enough to take the required action for it, and eventually you start feeling that you don't have the potential or ability to make that kind of money.

It's like being in a state of paralysis where you want to take action, but you just can't. I have been in these situations and I am sure even you have, haven't you? Even though these situations make you feel like you don't have the potential, the fact is that we always have unlimited potential. But the realization of your potential depends on your beliefs.

If you have conviction, it helps in unleashing your potential which motivates you to take action and eventually creates the results of your vision. Negative beliefs on the other hand, do not release potential and limits motivation to act, thereby do not provide any results.

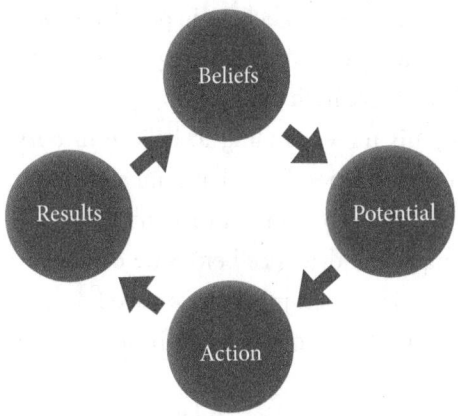

Beliefs are Vital for Tapping into Our Inner Potential and Realizing Our Visions

To understand this better, think of the best racing car in the world, with extraordinary potential and imagine driving and racing this car with the hand brakes on. Even though the car has great potential, it will not win the race since you have the hand brakes on. For the car to run at its best potential, you must release the hand brakes first. The moment you do that you will be surprised and probably even get scared of the speed at which the car can run.

A great author called Marianne Williamson once wrote: 'Our deepest fear is not that we are inadequate; our deepest fear is that we are powerful beyond measure.'

Driving with the hand brakes on is the same as having a vision without believing in it. So if you truly want to realize your highest potential, then start believing in your vision before it's too late. In my leadership workshops, people ask me how can we believe in ourselves when we have never seen any evidence of our potential in a particular area. In fact, how can we believe, if all we have seen is only negative evidence that we can't do something?

This is critical, most people in the world think that in order to believe in something you need to see it first. So they say: 'seeing is believing'. We use this understanding to even believe in people, by saying that when we see them keeping their commitments or when we see them performing, only then we can believe in them.

We even use this understanding to believe in ourselves by saying: 'I will invest in myself when I see that I am showing the dedication to create results.' We all keep living in this bubble of 'seeing is believing', and keep waiting to see evidence before we can believe in something. However believing in something after you see it is not called belief, it's called facing reality. This whole 'seeing is believing' concept is incorrect understanding.

Let us understand what belief is: 'Believing is seeing' would be more apt to define beliefs; which means that belief comes first and then comes seeing. Whatever you believe in, starts showing up in your life and so you can see it. A great example of this is the story of a legend called Walt Disney.

Walt Disney had the vision of creating Disney Land. A lot of people did not believe in his dream simply because they had never seen or heard of a project like it, so it was difficult for most people to believe in it. But Disney was a leader, and knew that seeing is not believing; rather believing is seeing. So he continued to believe in his vision, and eventually got the Disney Land project.

By the time Disney Land was inaugurated, Walt Disney was dead. He could not see his vision being realized. After the inauguration in October 1971, a reporter asked Roy Disney how he was feeling, since his brother Walt Disney could not get to see the opening of Disney Land. Roy paused for a moment and said: 'Walt saw it and that is why you are seeing it.'

Question is where did Walt see it? – He saw it in his vision and believed in it long before it was created in reality.

This is what separates leaders from ordinary people. Leaders have the ability to believe in things without any evidence. How do they do that? How do they believe in something without evidence? Pretty simple, they create belief with imagination. That's right, beliefs are created with imagination. When you don't have an external reality to help you believe in something, you can start by creating your own internal reality with the help of imagination. Your imagination is the world of your internal reality. Anything and everything is possible in the world of your imagination. I invite you to experience the power of your imagination.

As you are reading this, imagine that you have won the best leader's award in your organization and people are clapping for you. As you walk down the stage after receiving your award, people are congratulating you and you are feeling extremely proud and excited at the same time. Imagine the excitement and thrill you feel in this moment.

What you just did was an example of imagination. If you repeat this visualization, eventually it becomes a belief in your internal reality. Once it becomes a belief it releases your potential to release your motivation to take action and thus gives you the results of your vision.

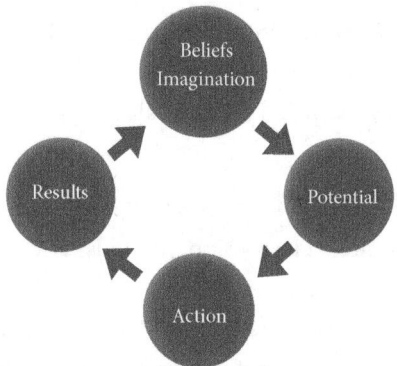

Imagination is the Power that Fires Our Beliefs

I have personally used this technique to create beliefs in many things about myself and so I have been able to create extraordinary results in my life too. Today I am an internationally famous leadership trainer, but I started believing in this vision much before it became reality.

Now it's your turn to believe in your vision by imagining that it is already achieved.

For a guided process of believing in your vision, log on to my website and download a free audio programme which I have specially designed for this purpose. This is a free gift for you since you have come this far in your leadership journey.

Chapter Summary

▶ Vision is the ability to consciously create a goal and visualize that the goal is already achieved.

▶ Most people are afraid to create a clear vision because they fear failure.

▶ Success is not only by chance, it is also a science.

▶ The most important part of the science of success is to firstly have a clear vision of your goal. And here are some simple steps for that:

- Create a vision which is clear and specific.
- Write the vision in visible places.
- Believe in your vision as if it is already achieved through daily visualization.
- Take strategic action.

▶ Once you create a clear vision, you must also believe in it passionately.

▶ Driving with the hand brakes on is the same as having a vision without believing in it. So if you truly want to realize your highest potential, then start believing in your vision before it is too late.

▶ Believing is seeing.

▶ Leaders have the ability to believe in things without any evidence.

▶ Beliefs can be created through imagination.

7

Values – The Source of Power

If you think of leaders like Steve Jobs, Mahatma Gandhi, Narayan Murthy, Warren Buffet, Ratan Tata, Mother Teresa or any other great leaders in the world, you will find one thing in common among all of them, and that is Power.

The greatest gift of leaders is their power. Look back in history, and think of any leader and you will see that they all had access to power. It is their power that made them stand out in a crowd; it is their power that got them success, got them the attention and admiration of millions in the world; it is their power that gave them the ability to establish a relationship with anyone they wanted. It is power that gave them the ability to be calm, even in the midst of chaos. It is their power, because of which leaders can achieve almost anything they want to.

Bad luck could not stop them, failures could not break them, problems could not limit them, infact nothing could come in the way of their success, because of the power they had. I was always curious about what the source of their power is! Why is it when everyone gives up, leaders still go on? How is it when nothing supports them, they still stand strong?

After many years of work and research, I finally discovered the source of their power. The moment I discovered the source, I started accessing it myself and started applying it in every area of my life. As a result, my success skyrocketed in every aspect of my life. It's as if I had access to unlimited power. In this chapter my deepest intention, is to share with you that source of unlimited power, so that you can also use it to get anything you want, in any area of your life.

First let's define power. Is it money, time, information, people, connections, knowledge, good luck? What exactly is it?

My definition of power is

Power = A person's ability to access and focus all internal power resources towards any desire.

What are internal power resources? As the term suggests, they are our internal resources that give us power, they are things like:

- Our ability to work hard
- To be dedicated towards something
- Being sincere
- Thinking creatively
- Devoting time
- Being motivated
- Being inspired
- Being focused

All internal resources which help you gain power to achieve your goals are known as internal power resources. When you have the ability to access and focus all such internal power resources for any desire, that is power. The fact is that we always have these internal power resources, but sometimes they are blocked and that's when we are unable to access these power resources. Once our power resources are blocked, automatically our weak resources come into action. Our internal weak resources are things which make us –

- Lazy
- Procrastinate

- Forgetful
- Make excuses
- Casual
- De-motivated
- Unable to think clearly and so on

These weak resources make us powerless and that is why sometimes even though we want to produce great results, we find ourselves powerless. Haven't you ever thought of why you don't have the motivation to work on something you have been wanting for a long time? Losing weight, for example?

On the other hand, leaders are powerful because they know how to access their internal power resources and focus them towards any desired goal. Ordinary people are unable to do this consciously, and so find themselves powerless on many occasions. But I am sure you would agree, that if you had the ability to access your internal power resources by choice, it would be like having access to unlimited power, right? Well, the good news is, that this unlimited power is always within us, you just have to learn to access it by choice.

People often ask me questions like-why are we able to access our power resources only in some areas of life, while in some areas we are weak and powerless? Why is it that we are extremely hard working and focused in some areas, and yet extremely lazy and unfocused in others? The answer to these questions lies in the source of unlimited power which you are about to discover now.

The source of unlimited power is consciously working as per our highest values

The source of power is working consciously in tandem with our highest values, every day of our lives. What I have discovered is that whenever we work as per our highest values, we automatically become powerful and gain access to all our internal power resources. We suddenly become hard-working, dedicated, sincere, focused and creative; we find a lot of time for what we love to do.

But the moment we work according to our lowest values, we automatically become weak and powerless and subsequently become lazy, procrastinate, become forgetful, make excuses, lose focus and so on.

Working as per our highest values = power (Access to all our internal power resources)

Working as per our lowest values = powerlessness (Lose access to all our internal power resources)

The unfortunate part is that most people today, are not even clear about their highest values. It is because of this that most people end up working as per their lowest values in life.

If I ask you to write down a list of your exact values in the hierarchy of what's most important to you in just one minute, will you be able to give me a clear list of all your values?

In all probability like most people, you will not be able to answer this question immediately. (And if you are able to, then I must congratulate you, because then you are truly living a powerful life.) I say this because most people in the world are not even clear about their values. And when we are not clear of our highest values, then our life automatically gets driven by our lowest values, making us powerless.

Look at life like driving a car. In order to drive a car, we must always be absolutely clear about where we are going and in how much time we need to reach there. When we become distracted while driving, then we take wrong turns, we stop unnecessarily during the journey; we may reach the wrong destination and the worst part of being distracted while driving is that we can even have accidents.

The same thing happens to us when we are not clear of our highest values. We make wrong decisions; we become lazy in areas where we need to work the hardest; we take the most important people in our life for granted and give more importance to people who are not even important in our life; and we even have accidents in life.

On the other hand leaders are people, who always have complete clarity about their values. They live everyday consciously as per their highest values; that's what gives them power. That is why leaders are always able to access and focus all their internal power resources towards their desired goals. But ordinary people keep struggling, they become weak and powerless in their lives, since they are unable to access and focus their power resources towards their desired goals.

When the leaders of an organization are clear of their own values, then they are able to steer the organization in the right direction by also helping their employees to work as per the highest values of the organization. But again, unfortunately most organizations and their employees are not clear of their highest values.

If you don't believe me, ask this question to your team: *What are the highest values of our organization? Do you work every day consciously in alignment with those values?* I bet that you will hardly find any person in your team who is 100% clear about the organizational values; and if they are, they may not be working 100% in alignment with those values. This is the reasons most organizations don't become market leaders.

Organizations like Apple which are market leaders, are always conscious of working as per their highest values. In fact they work so much in alignment with their highest values, that even their customers know their values.

For example, can you tell me what the highest values of Apple are?

I am sure you would think of words like Quality Excellence, Design Excellence and Innovation.

When people or organizations consciously work as per their highest values, then people around them can clearly see and identify those values.

The bottom line is that the source of ultimate power for leaders is their ability to consciously work in alignment of their highest values. This gives them the ability to access and focus all the internal power resources towards their desired goals and achieve them successfully.

What are values?

Values are the hierarchy of our highest to lowest priorities.

Think of the words that come to your mind when you hear the word 'value'. Here is a list of words that I get from participants during my leadership workshops:

▶ Important
▶ Priorities
▶ What we are serious about
▶ Highest interests

When you say something is valuable to you, you may also say it is very important to you; it is your highest priority or that you are extremely serious about it. It is also fair to say that values are what you give high or low priority or importance to. Thus I am defining values as the hierarchy of our highest to lowest priorities. We have two types of values – High Values and Low Values.

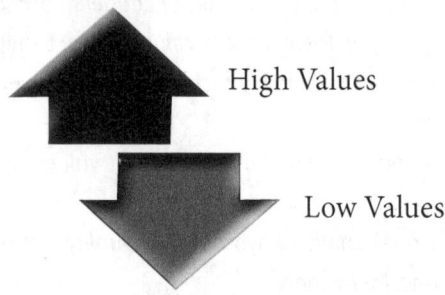

High Values

Low Values

High values and low values can also be interpreted as **High Importance and Low Importance** or **High Priority and Low Priority.** It is our values that determine whether we have the motivation to take action or procrastinate; whether we get along with people or not; how much money we make; how successful we are – everything depends on our values. It is our values that give us our direction, our destination and eventually our destiny. We know this is true because we have already learnt that: **Whenever we work as per our highest values, we automatically have access to all our internal power resources like –**

► Hard work
► Sincerity
► Dedication
► Ample time
► Creativity
► Focus
► Confidence
► Inspiration
► Motivation
► Patience
► Excellent Memory
► Sensitivity
► Awareness
► Abundant Energy

On the other hand, whenever we work as per our lowest values we lose access to our internal resources. We become –

► Lazy
► Insincere
► Distracted
► Confused
► Un-focused
► De-motivated
► Impatient
► Forgetful

▶ Insensitive
▶ Unaware
▶ Tired

In essence, if you are clear and consciously work as per your highest values, your power increases and, if you are unclear and work as per your lower values, your power decreases.

For example, I often meet people who tell me that their children are lazy, but I tell them that there is no such thing as a lazy child or a lazy person. You may also feel that you are a lazy person or know someone who you consider to be a lazy person. To this, I repeat, with absolute certainty, that there is no such thing as a lazy person; it's only a matter of values.

You will notice that when a child is playing or watching television or doing anything that is of high interest to him, the same lazy child has access to all their internal power resources like hard work, sincerity, dedication, creativity, focus and motivation. Have you ever seen a child playing video games? You will notice that even if he loses the game, he never loses patience; he plays again and again until he wins the game. While playing, he is completely focused; he never gets tired and can go on for hours if you don't stop him.

The same child, when asked to do his school homework, loses access to his internal power resources and becomes lazy, tired and irritated and avoids doing the homework. How is it that the same child, who has power to take consistent action in one area, is completely lazy in another? It's because when human beings work as per their highest values, their power increases, but when they work as per their lowest values, their power decreases drastically.

Now that you have understood how values are connected with power, there is one more critical thing about values that you must understand.

We always have a hierarchy of values, from what's highest on our priorities to what's lowest on our priorities. Making a small shift in this hierarchy can completely transform the way we live our lives.

When I was conducting a leadership workshop for a multinational organization, we worked on their current hierarchy of values (using our values identifier test which you will learn about in this chapter) and this is what we discovered:

► *Profitability*
► *Satisfied employees*
► *Working as per rules*
► *Customer service*

This organization was struggling with a lot of their projects because their customers were not happy with them. Looking at their hierarchy of values, it was evident that their customers were unhappy because customer satisfaction was at the bottom of their priorities. Whenever there was a choice between focusing between profitability and customer service, they would usually choose profitability. They were quite shocked when they saw this hierarchy as a result of using my Values Identifier Test. They had thought customer service was always their highest priority but obviously, they were wrong. This is a classic example of not being clear about our highest values.

I eventually helped the top management make a shift in the hierarchy of their values, as a result of which they saw remarkable growth in their customer satisfaction surveys.

What you think is your highest desire may not necessarily be your highest value. It is a myth that I want to break for individuals and organizations – our highest desires may not necessarily be our highest values. I call these desires our 'low value desires' and when we live our lives as per our low values, we become weak and powerless. Here is an example of a CEO who discovered this during my executive coaching session.

The CEO said to me: 'I truly desire to give more time to my family and have fulfilling relationships at home; but no matter what I do, I am becoming more and more powerless at home. I have very little time for family. My relationships with my wife and children are getting worse. Why is it that, in spite of being so successful and powerful at work, I am so powerless at home?'

I asked him, 'First you tell me what is more important to you in your values, your family or your work?'

His answer was, 'My family is definitely my first priority, which is why I work so hard, so that I can give them the best'. Then we conducted the values identifier test on him and discovered his real values. This is how they looked:

▶ *Work*
▶ *Travelling for work*
▶ *Networking for more business*
▶ *Children*
▶ *Wife*
▶ *Parents*

It was clear that, though he truly desired to give more time to his family, family was his lowest value desire. And since they came low in his hierarchy, he was powerless in that area. Powerless as in, when it came to his family, he had very little access to his internal power resources. Thus, he never found time for them and had very little patience to interact with them. He couldn't be creative in solving problems with his wife. It was as if the CEO was not the same person at home.

In this coaching session I was able to help the CEO resolve this situation by creating clarity and helping him redesign the hierarchy of his values consciously. We did what I call my Redesigning Values Exercise (you will learn this exercise in this chapter). With the help of this exercise, he was able to create clarity and put his family above work on the hierarchy of his values. The moment he did that, he felt powerful and immediately, had access to focus all his internal power resources towards his family. All his power resources like hard work, sincerity, dedication, time, creativity, focus, patience and energy became available to him for his family.

As a result of this, in the coaching session itself, he was able to see creative solutions for a lot of the problems related to his family, which he could not see earlier. He was suddenly clear on how to resolve the conflicts with his wife and recreate a beautiful relationship with her. He felt as powerful about his family now, as he did about work. It was almost like magic. That's the power of consciously living your life as per your highest values instead of unconsciously living as per your low value desires.

Just a few days after that, in our next coaching session, his wife came to meet me because she wanted to know what magic I had done on her husband. She said he had suddenly become the person she knew and got married to ten years back. I shared with her the importance of values and then we did the values identifier test with her as well. She was shocked at how her husband actually came low in her values, while her house and children came higher on her values. Then we did the redesigning values exercise with her and she was surprised at how easy it was to solve her relationship issues, after placing her husband highest on her values.

After a couple of months, the CEO asked me to conduct the same session with his entire team. It completely transformed his team.

The *Values Identifier Test* and the *Redesigning Values Exercise*, which can help you identify your current values and then redesign the hierarchy of your values. These exercises will give you power to access and focus all your internal power resources towards any area of your life. You can use this test and exercise for yourself, your family or even the entire team in the organization.

Values Identifier Test – for high values

In order to identify your actual values hierarchy, answer the following questions honestly

1. What are the areas in which you can easily find time?
2. What are the areas in which you are able to spend maximum money?
3. What are the areas in which you are most hard working?
4. What are the areas in which you are most sincere?
5. What are the areas in which you are most dedicated?
6. What are the areas in which you are most creative?
7. What are the areas in which you are most focused in life?
8. What are the areas in which you have maximum patience?
9. What are the areas in which you are most confident?
10. What are the areas in which you are most inspired?
11. What are the areas in which you are most motivated to take action?
12. What are the areas in which you are most sensitive?
13. What are the areas in which you have lots of energy?
14 What are the areas in which you are most organized?
15. What are the areas for which you regularly create short term and long-term goals?
16. What are the areas in which you have good memory?

After you complete answering the above questions, count how many times any area has repeated itself in the list of answers. This is part one of the test, which is only for identifying high values; so only mention those areas where you truly find the maximum of your internal power resources.

To make it easy for you to answer the above questions, I have given a table below where all the resources are given in the first column the rest of the columns are different areas of your life. I have provided four columns, but you can increase the number of columns if you need to. Ask yourself if you find time for an area e.g. clients. If you always find time for your clients then simply put a tick mark against it.

Here is an example of a test taken by a senior manager, let's call him John, who was attending my leadership workshop

	Internal Power Resources	Clients	Office	Meetings	Making Money	Wife
1	Find time	√	√	√	√	√
2	Spend money	√	√			√
3	Hard working	√	√	√	√	√
4	Sincere	√	√	√	√	√
5	Dedicated	√	√	√	√	√
6	Creative	√	√	√	√	√
7	Focused	√	√	√		
8	Patience	√	√	√		√
9	Confident	√	√	√	√	√
10	Inspired	√	√	√	√	
11	Motivated	√	√	√	√	√
12	Sensitive/ Aware	√	√	√	√	
13	Have lots of energy	√	√	√		
14	Organized	√	√	√	√	

15	Make goals	√	√	√	√	
16	Have good memory	√	√	√	√	
Total		16	16	15	11	12

As per the above scores, the following is the hierarchy of John's actual highest values:

1. Office – 16
2. Clients – 16
3. Meetings – 15
4. Wife – 12
5. Making money – 11

Anything less than ten points does not qualify to be one of your high values. If you have a tie between two areas, then you must decide by asking yourself, which area you give more or less time or money or dedication to, and then decide the hierarchy accordingly. Like in John's case, although office and clients both have 16 points, he personally knew that he gave more time and energy to the office than the clients and thus, he decided that office was his first and clients were his second highest value. Giving his wife 12 points and making money 11 points, it does not mean that his wife or making money are low in his values, as anything which is higher than 10 points is qualified to be the highest values.

These are all the areas where John has a lot of power, because he is able to access most of his internal power resources for them. Thus, in these areas, his ability to take action and to create results is very powerful. Now let's find out John's lower values hierarchy from the second part of this test –

Values Identifier Test – for low values

In order to identify your actual low values hierarchy, answer the following questions honestly

1. What are the areas in which you have little time?
2. What are the areas in which you hardly spend money?
3. What are the areas in which you are lazy and procrastinate?
4. What are the areas in which you find yourself indifferent?
5. What are the areas in which you are less dedicated?
6. What are the areas in which you find yourself being stuck and confused?
7. What are the areas in which you constantly lose focus?
8. What are the areas in which you are very impatient?
9. What are the areas in which you lack confidence?
10. What are the areas in which you are not inspired to take action?
11 What are the areas in which you keep getting de-motivated?
12. What are the areas in which you are less sensitive?
13. What are the areas in which you get tired very easily?
14. What are the areas in which you are unorganized?
15. What are the areas in which you don't make goals?
16. What are the areas in which you are very forgetful?

Again here is John's list of low values where in the first column there is a list of his internal weak resources and then the rest of the areas where he demonstrates these weak resources:

	Internal Weak Resources	Exercising	Meditation	Parents	Writing blog	Selling
1	Does not find time	√	√	√	√	√

2	Hardly spends money	√	√			
3	Lazy/Procras-tinates	√	√	√	√	√
4	Causal	√	√	√		√
5	Less Dedicated	√	√	√	√	√
6	Stuck and confused	√			√	√
7	Defocused	√	√	√		√
8	Impatient	√				√
9	Lack confidence	√		√	√	
10	Uninspired to take action	√	√	√	√	√
11	De-motivated	√	√	√	√	√
12	Less sensitive	√	√	√	√	√
13	Get tired easily	√	√	√	√	√
14	Unorganized	√	√	√	√	√
15	Don't make goals	√	√	√	√	√
16	Forgetful	√	√	√	√	√
Total		16 − 16 = 0	16 − 14 = 2	16 − 13 = 3	16 − 14 = 2	16 − 12 = 4

Make sure you subtract the final score from 16. That would give you the score for your lowest values hierarchy. Now if I take John's highest and lowest values scores and put them together, here is how it looks:

John's high values hierarchy

1	Office	16
2	Clients	16
3	Meetings	15
4	Wife	12
5	Making money	11

John's low values hierarchy

6	Selling	4
7	Parents	3
8	Writing blog	2
9	Meditation	2
10	Exercise	0

Your Values Identifier Test – High Values

	Internal Power Resources					
1	Find time					
2	Spend money					

3	Hard working					
4	Sincere					
5	Dedicated					
6	Creative					
7	Focused					
8	Patience					
9	Confident					
10	Inspired					
11	Motivated					
12	Sensitive/Aware					
13	Have lots of energy					
14	Organized					
15	Make goals					
16	Have good memory					
Total						

Your Values Identifier test – Low Values

	Internal Weak Resources					
1	Does not find time					

2	Hardly spends money					
3	Lazy/ Procrastinates					
4	Causal					
5	Less Dedicated					
6	Stuck and confused					
7	Defocused					
8	Impatient					
9	Lack confidence					
10	Uninspired to take action					
11	De-motivated					
12	Less sensitive					
13	Get tired easily					
14	Unorganized					
15	Don't make goals					
16	Forgetful					
Total						

Analysis of the values hierarchy

1. **Check whether your highest values are in alignment or in conflict with your highest desires/goals.**

   Most people, when they take this values identifier test realize that there is a huge conflict between their highest values and their highest desires and goals, and this leads to frustration.

   When I asked this question to John, he said some of his highest desires were:

   • To give a lot of time to his old parents.
   • To exercise regularly, for taking care of his back pain.
   • To meditate in order to manage the stress in his life.

   Even though John desired these things, he was unable to take consistent action for any of them. In fact, he found himself quite weak and powerless. The reason was simple – if you look at his values hierarchy, all his values are completely in conflict with his desires; in fact his desires have become his low values. The consequences were that John was feeling a lot of frustration, helplessness, guilt and stress. All these negative feelings were spreading to impact the other areas of John's higher values and thus, his productivity in his high value areas was also reducing. This is what happens when our highest values are in conflict with our highest desires, so check if your own values are in alignment or in conflict with your highest desires.

2. **Check if you still desire your low values?**

   If you have many low values in your hierarchy, which are still your desires, then that will increase the frustration in your life. You must either stop desiring them or delegate them or shift them to your highest values.

If you are clear that your low values are truly not important to you, then stop desiring them and they will stop troubling you. If you delegate them, that is you hand them over to someone else then again they will stop troubling you.

If you shift them to your higher values hierarchy consciously, then you will achieve them and it would make you feel happy and successful.

But if you continue to desire them, yet keep them in your low values, you will definitely feel weak and helpless. So check if you still desire your low values and take one of the three actions above to make sure you are not losing energy in these low value desires.

3. **Check if there are too many values tied to each other.**

Among all those values where there is a tie, that is you get the same scoring for two or more values, then you will find yourself struggling to prioritize between them.

Like in John's case, there is a tie between his office and his clients. It is the area which will always put him under pressure, when he has to prioritize between attending regular office and meeting clients. To reduce the struggle in this area, all he needs to do is clearly identify which one is more important, so that while making decisions he can be clear about where to sacrifice and where to focus.

Great leaders are people who are able to clearly take a conscious decision between such values and thus, able to make difficult decisions quickly and easily. If you find yourself torn between two things regularly in your life, then you must take a conscious choice between them for living a life of power.

A perfect example for this in India is, when a man gets married he usually finds himself struggling between his wife and his mother. This is a common reality that creates stress for most Indian men. In my own life, this used to be an area where I struggled, but after I redesigned my values consciously, the struggle was over. I consciously realized that it is not practical for me to give more time to my mother over my wife; so I consciously decided to put my wife on a higher priority.

This is a difficult decision but it's necessary for a life of power. At the same time, it would be unjust to my mother if I keep her in my low values. So she certainly remains on my highest values list, but now I know that in the hierarchy of my highest values, my wife comes first and then my mother.

This made it easy for me to make decisions when there was a conflict between both of them. However, many people unconsciously end up keeping their parents in their low values and have very little time for them. If you see, even in John's values hierarchy, parents come at the lower end of his hierarchy, which creates a lot of stress between him and his parents.

So, ask yourself, are there too many values which have a tie between them?

4. **Check if your values are helping you meet your End Value Emotions such as happiness, satisfaction and fulfillment.**

All our values are simply a means to reach certain end value emotions. We value something because it gives us some emotional fulfillment at the end of it. For example:

- We value office work, because we value the end emotions of success and achievement
- We value our family, because we value end emotions like love and happiness
- When we value money, it's because we value end emotions like security and abundance

Similarly, everything we do in life gives us certain end emotions that we value the most. Ask yourself – if you are about to die, which emotions would you value the most? Even if you make a lot of money and grow to be very successful, would you like to die unhappy, unsatisfied and unfulfilled? I am sure you wouldn't like that! Thus, I like to believe that the highest end value for every person is emotions like happiness, satisfaction and fulfillment. Check if your values are helping you meet these end value emotions.

Most people spend their entire lives valuing things that make them feel emotions like success, adventure, excitement and the like. While success is not a low value emotion, if in your hierarchy of values, it is higher than happiness, then that is a problem.

Happy people can be successful but successful people are not necessarily happy. The movie, *3 Idiots* is a perfect example of this. In the film Amir Khan says that one shouldn't run behind success; instead one should do what makes one happy and then success is sure to run behind you. So, are your values helping you feel all of your end value emotions?

5. **Check if your values are in alignment or in conflict with the values of your organization and with the values of people who are closest to you.**

This is the most critical part of values; when our highest values are in conflict with those of our organization, or with people who are closest to us, the quality of our life deteriorates. For instance, John's highest values were completely in conflict with his wife's values. Here is a comparison of his value hierarchy vs his wife's values hierarchy

John's Values	His Wife's Values
Office	Children
Clients	Home

Meetings	Socializing
Wife	In-Laws
Making money	Husband
Sales	Hobbies
Parents	Career
Blogging	Meditation
Meditation	Exercising
Exercise	Making money

The above list shows that there was practically no alignment between their highest values and thus, there were many conflicts in their relationship. If John wants to have a happy marriage, he must sit with his wife and create alignment between their values through open communication.

Just because some people have different values, does not mean that they cannot get along with each other. What matters is that they are clear about each other's values and that they have reasonable expectations of each other, based on clarity of those values.

During my leadership workshops, I help people understand their team-mates better by encouraging them to have more clarity regarding each other's values, and then having reasonable expectations based on that clarity. I have taken teams that were in complete conflict with each other, and been able to help them create harmony in their relationships by helping them align their values with each other.

So, ask yourself if your highest values are in alignment or in conflict with your organizational values and with the values of the people closest in your life.

The quality of your life depends on the hierarchy of your values. For example, what if I exchange John's value of office from first to fourth position and shift the value of his wife from fourth to first position? Do you think that would change the quality of his life? What if I replace meditation with making money, would that make a difference in his life?

What if an organization like Apple values profitability more than design excellence? What if Mother Teresa would have valued making money more than love and peace? What if a country values peace more than the growth of its territory? What if a country values ethics more than growth? What if people value happiness more than success?

Making small changes in our individual or organizational values hierarchy can completely change the quality of our lives. Learn how to consciously redesign your values through the **Redesigning Values Exercise.**

1. **Make a choice** – of your values hierarchy based on the following rules:

    *   Make sure they are aligned with the highest desires/goals of your life.
    *   Make sure that what is on your low values hierarchy is not important to you.
    *   Make sure there is a clear distinction between each value in terms of the hierarchy (I know this is a tough decision, but you must take this decision for a powerful life).
    *   Make sure your highest values are in alignment with your end value emotions like happiness, satisfaction and fulfillment.
    *   Make sure your highest values are in alignment with the

values of your organization and those of the people closest in your life.

2. **Daily Conditioning** – Once you have made a choice of your new values hierarchy, now you need to condition it, so that it is programmed in your subconscious mind. You must reach a point where you start acting as per your new values subconsciously, so that they become an integral part of your life, just like your current values.

Following are the steps that you need to follow in order to condition the new values:

a. Every morning, start your day by reading your new values hierarchy with the following statements:

'These are the highest values of my life that I have consciously chosen and thus, even today I choose to honour them by acting in alignment with my highest values. I may not brush my teeth, have my food, or even bathe today, but I will definitely remember to live as per the highest values of my conscious choice. I will make whatever sacrifice is necessary today and every day to live as per the highest values of my conscious choice. I will give my best today, to live as per my highest values of my choice.'

Read these statements with full emotional intensity then re-read your new values once again.

3. **Associate pleasure with your new values** – In order to redesign your values, you must understand the two psychological needs of all human beings. These are not just values, but human needs. Just like we have basic needs like breathing, food, water, we also have two basic psychological needs:

1. Our need to avoid pain, and
2. Our need to gain pleasure.

Whatever is higher on our hierarchy of values, it's because we feel it gives us great pleasure and whatever is lower on our hierarchy of values, it's because we feel it gives us pain and thus we avoid those things.

For example, I spent the maximum time of my life reading and researching on human behaviour because, at a very early age, I realized that if I learn the secret to human behaviour then I could learn the secrets of success and happiness. I connected learning human behaviour with lots of pleasure. Hence, I always had energy and time for reading psychology books and attending any seminars or workshops that could help me learn more about human behaviour.

For a long time in life, I avoided exercise because of a childhood memory of going to a gym to exercise, overdoing some weight lifting and hurting myself. The next morning, when I got up I realized I could not walk and I had immense pain in my legs and hands. That pain lasted for almost a week and it left a great impact on me and thus, I connected exercising with lot of pain. For many years I avoided exercising, even though I knew it was good for me.

I had friends who hated reading psychology books, studying human behaviour or attending human behaviour seminars and workshops. They found it a complete waste of time. That's because they always felt psychology was the study of mentally sick people. They also thought that the people who went for human behaviour workshops were those who had a problem with their own behaviour. So, for them, learning about human behaviour meant pain and they always avoided such workshops.

I also found friends who loved exercising every single day. Somehow, they always had the time and energy to go to the gym every day and exercise for at least one hour, rigorously. That's because they felt keeping fit and healthy helped them feel confident

about themselves and also made them attractive enough to get a
date. Thus, for them, exercising everyday meant pleasure.

I am sure you have seen this around you as well. What gives pleasure to you, may be painful for someone else, and what gives pain to you may be pleasure for someone else!

This tells us that our experiences of pain and pleasure are mostly based on our perception. It is our perception that make something an experience of pain or pleasure. Which means if we control our perception, we can control what gives us pain or pleasure and if we can control what gives us pain or pleasure, we can control what we value more or less.

When we were children, our parents, friends, teachers and society shaped our perception of pain and pleasure. As we grew up, our perceptions of what meant pain and pleasure were further influenced by our office environment, colleagues, bosses, spouse, relatives and so on. Thus, most human beings live their lives with perceptions of pain and pleasure given by others; these become their high or low values and they think of it as a reality, they think they have no choice in redesigning their values. You will hear people saying, 'That's the way I am, I can't help it'.

Leaders understand that we always have a choice of what gives pain or pleasure. Our mind has so much power that when we change our meanings about things, we can change whether it gives us pain or pleasure. A very powerful example of this is the fire-walk exercise that we do in my workshops.

When people come to know that they are supposed to walk on fire, at first they object strongly, because they know that fire means pain. But after I do a one-hour perception change power talk with the group, it alters their perception of fire so drastically that they then feel walking on fire is going to be the best thing in the world.

They then feel fire-walking will give them pleasure and thus the same people who refused to do it an hour ago, cannot wait to walk on fire. This is not a one-time experience; I've witnessed it at every single fire-walk session that I do for groups, in various organizations all over the world. It is thus possible to re-design your values by re-conditioning what you associate pain or pleasure with.

People ask me whether I hypnotize the group before they walk on fire. Well of course not! All I do is, give people the ability to control their perceptions. When they change their perceptions they are able to feel pleasure in walking on fire, instead of pain. As a result of this exercise, participants learn to change their perceptions about fear of failure and achieving seemingly impossible goals.

I have trained thousands of executives from many organizations who believed their goals could not be achieved because they were too difficult due to the market conditions or due to lack of resources or due to lack of skills, or simply because they thought it was an unpractical goal. After one fire-walk training session, these people achieved their goals simply because they were able to associate pleasure to difficult goals rather than pain.

Amongst many such is one example of an organization called Piramal Healthcare, which had a target, which seemed impossible to their 2,500 sales representatives. With our fire-walk session, not only did they achieve their goal once but twice, in two consecutive years. (You can read more about the study here http://www.miteshkhatri.com/case-studies/piramal-health-care-true-care/)

4. Now you have learnt three effective ways of redesigning your values: 1) Making a choice, 2) Daily conditioning and 3) Associating pleasure with your new values. If you truly want to change your values hierarchy, then you would also need a personal coach to support you. Getting a personal coach is the fastest and the easiest

way to redesign your new values. Look at the best performers in the world in any area of life; they all have a coach. Whether it is a great cricket player like Sachin Tendulkar, a very successful business tycoon like Richard Branson, a great dancer like Shiamak Davar. Every great leader, in any area, has a coach from whom they learn their skills.

The job of the coach is to simply push you, encourage you and motivate you to constantly keep working as per your highest values hierarchy by choice. I have had a personal coach for the last ten years now, who has helped me to always stay on track with my highest values hierarchy. A personal coach creates accountability and without accountability, there are chances that we might slip into our lower values of life. If you truly mean to live as per your highest values, then investing money to get a personal coach is the first way to demonstrate that you truly value it. You only spend on what is truly valuable for you and if you find yourself not willing to spend on your new values then you haven't really committed to them yet.

If you follow the above given steps of the Redesigning Values Exercise, you can live a life of your choice, instead of one that is designed by your circumstances. Remember, if you don't consciously live by your highest values then you would naturally gravitate towards your lowest values, so start every morning by consciously focusing on your highest values and living by them.

If you would like to have a personal coaching session to do this exercise, write to me at mitesh@guidinglightindia.com. With our expert in-house coaching, this exercise can become a life-long asset. For now, please do this exercise on your own and do e-mail me your results, I would love to hear from you, about how you have redesigned your life by redesigning your values.

Chapter Summary

▶ Values can give you unlimited power.

▶ Power = A person's ability to access and focus all internal power resources towards any desire.

▶ All internal resources that help you gain power to achieve your goals are known as internal power resources.

▶ The source of unlimited power is consciously working as per our highest values.

▶ If you are clear about your values, and consciously work as per your highest values, your power increases. If you are unclear and work as per your lower values, your power decreases.

▶ Making a small shift in this hierarchy can completely transform the way we live our lives.

▶ Use the Values Identifier Test to identify your values.

▶ Analysis of your values hierarchy:

  1. Check if your highest values are in alignment or in conflict with your highest desires/goals.

  2. Check if you still desire your low values.

  3. Check if there are too many values tied to each other.

  4. Check if your values are helping you meet your end value emotions such as happiness, satisfaction and fulfilment.

  5. Check if your values are in alignment or in conflict with the values of your organization and with the values of people who are closest to you.

▶ You always have a choice to redesign your values by using the following steps:

  1. Make a choice.

  2. Daily Conditioning.

  3. Associate pleasure with your new values.

8

Mastering Time – Achieving More in Less Time

Ordinary people achieve less things in more time, whereas leaders achieve more things in less time

I am sure you would agree that there is a big difference between the productivity levels of an ordinary person, when compared to that of an extraordinary leader. Take any ordinary person, and you will find that they take years to achieve what extraordinary leaders achieve in only months.

So here comes the important question – why are extraordinary leaders more productive than ordinary people? This time the answer is simple – **Ordinary people are less productive because they are poor time managers; leaders are super productive because they master time management.**

Leaders are super productive because they know how to manage both themselves as well as their time. It is possible to fulfil your dreams in just months instead of years, by mastering the art of time management. This art however can be honed by anyone. All it requires is perseverance and persistence at practicing the principles which I will share with you in this chapter.

One of the key reasons ordinary people are poor at time management is because they manage time reactively without any time management *system*. Leaders have mastery over time management simply because they follow a time management system. I have asked many people in my workshops if they use a specific time management system. Almost always, people have said they do not. But watch a leader's life closely, and you will always find them using an effective time management system, which gives them control over time.

If you ask any ordinary person what they are doing next month, their answer would be – 'I am not sure, next month is too far'. Ask the same question to a leader, and he would look at his calendar and tell you what he is doing next month clearly! You see, ordinary people have no control over their present and future time and hence are less productive. Leaders have a lot of control over their present and future time and so are super productive.

It is important to understand that if you have no system in place, you have no control and if you have no control, you are not productive. It is a must to have a time management system if you want to be super productive like a leader.

Here is an example of a time management system, which I learnt in the course of working with hundreds of leaders over ten years. I call this system the SP System i.e. the Super Productivity System. It has three simple steps:

1. Visibility on paper
2. Prioritization according to values
3. Capturing immediately

Let's understand each of these steps in detail

1. Visibility on paper

When I ask people: 'Do you have a lot of work in your day-to-day life?' They respond saying yes, they have a lot of work. I am sure you would say the same if you were asked this question. I then go on to ask people these questions:

- Can you show me all your work?
- Do you have 100% visibility of all your work on paper at all times?
- Do you have a paper on which you have all your work written? And when I say all I really mean *all* your work written.

Most people tell me they have some work written in their to-do lists but not all their work. Many times I meet people who don't even have a to-do list; no visibility of their work on paper. Participants often ask me what the problem is, if we don't write all our work on paper. If our memories serve us well, we can remember most of our work. So then what is the need to write everything on 'paper'?

When you have lack of visibility on paper, it leads to the following problems:

1. You may forget to do things.
2. You may do things when it is too late.
3. You may do things which are not necessary.
4. You may take too long to do some things.
5. You may miss out on some very important work.
6. You may be under the illusion that there is no work.
7. You may be under the illusion that there is too much work.
8. You may be under stress of mostly doing things last minute.
9. You may be mostly reactive in doing your work instead of being proactive.
10. You may be unaware of how unproductive you are being.
11. You may be unaware that you are wasting a lot of time in your life.

The list just goes on and on. It does not take rocket science to understand that visibility is a basic necessity to do anything successfully. I play this simple game to explain the importance of visibility which I would like you to go through as well.

From wherever you are sitting, go to the entrance of your room and touch the door knob and come back. Now, you may think what a simple and silly game this is. But just play along with me, and I am sure you will enjoy the experiential learning of this concept of time management. So you need to get up, walk to one of the doors in your house, touch the door knob and come back, that's it.

You're back! Superb, great job! Now, do the same thing again, but this time, go with your eyes closed. And no cheating! Close your eyes and only then do the same task again.

Well, I am sure you realized that a simple task became a little difficult when I asked you to do it with your eyes closed. Is it not? The lesson from this game is really very simple – **The lack of visibility can make your life really difficult.**

Yet most people do not have any visibility of their work on paper. And it is because of this that they have very little control over their work and time. Thus, the first step in this Super Productivity System is to create 100% visibility of your work on paper. Is this the same as your to-do list? No it's not the same thing; because you may not be doing everything that you have written on a sheet of paper. A to-do list is only work which you definitely have to do, that's why it's called a to-do list. What I am talking about is simply visibility of all your work on paper.

While you read this chapter I would really like you to experience the power of the SP System, so please start by practicing the first step starting now. Take a notepad and start writing all the work you have in life ranging from your personal to professional tasks – everything.

When I ask participants in my workshop to do this first visibility exercise, they take minimum of an hour. Why? – Because you literally have to write everything. You won't understand the magnitude of this exercise until you really do it yourself. So I suggest you start writing now, and when you feel you have completed your list, use the following list as a reference and you will definitely have more things to write.

Visibility of all your work

This includes everything that you have to do in life

1	Things you said you would do	21	Organizing things at home
2	Things you were asked to do	22	Holiday and vacations to plan
3	Things you always wanted to do	23	Functions to attend
4	Things you left incomplete	24	Books to read
5	Things you gave up on	25	Websites to visit
6	Things you are avoiding	26	Workshops and courses to attend
7	Your to-do list	27	Deadlines to meet
8	Task list	28	Emergencies to attend to
9	Emails	29	Bills to pay
10	Memos to read and write	30	Taxes
11	Reports to go through	31	Shopping
12	Phone calls to make	32	Exercise
13	Phone calls to receive	33	Meditation
14	Voice mails to check	34	Sports

15	Check and send SMS messages	35	Personal Grooming
16	Meetings to attend	36	Time to spend with family
17	Scheduling your day	37	Personal time for yourself
18	Updating address book and contacts	38	Hobbies to pursue
19	Back up your computer data	39	Birthdays to remember
20	Expense and Budget reports	40	Celebrating auspicious days

I am sure if you do this exercise honestly, you will definitely have more than 50 tasks written in your notepad. As you look at all these tasks, what are your feelings and thoughts? I am sure you are experiencing thoughts and feelings such as:

- My God, so much to do!
- When will I ever do all this?
- Is it possible to ever finish all this?
- Tension
- Worry
- Disbelief
- Heavy-heartedness
- Pressure

Phew! You might be experiencing such and other similar thoughts or feelings. This is natural, but I promise you that by the time you practice all the three steps of the SP System in this chapter, you will be feeling very different. I promise! Just continue working with me here. Moving on to the second step of the SP System – prioritization.

Prioritizing according to values

Here is another question: 'If I give you two tasks, one which will take less time to finish, while another which will take more time to finish; which one will you prioritize first?'

Almost everyone in the workshop decided to prioritize the task which would take less time. This is the major reason why most people are poor time managers, because they usually prioritize tasks which take less time, rather than checking the priority level of the task.

If I ask the same question to leaders, the first question they ask is: *What's the priority level of these tasks? Does the priority align with my highest values?*

Only when they realize that these tasks are truly in alignment with their highest values, do they prioritize them. But most people never ask themselves the priority level of their tasks.

What is meant by priority levels? In the Super Productivity System we have three priority levels of any work –

1. **HP High Priority Level** (Aligned with the highest values and already scheduled)
2. **SP – Secondary Priority Level** (Aligned with highest values and willing to schedule)
3. **LP – Lowest Priority Level** (Not aligned with highest values and not willing to schedule)

Each of these priorities has specific criteria, and have to be understood correctly. So let us start with the first level:

HP – High Priority Level – A task is qualified as a HP only when it fulfils these two criteria:

1. **It has to be aligned with your highest values** – If a task is not aligned with your highest values, then you will never have the motivation and energy to work on it seriously. Besides if the task is not aligned with your values, it would not accomplish anything

that is worthy for you. Leaders are able to achieve more things in less time because they always prioritize those things which are aligned with their highest values.

Ordinary people waste a lot of time, because they unconsciously engage in a lot of work that is in conflict with their values. For example, my highest values are to be a Leadership and Transformational Trainer; be a best-selling author; have great relationships, financial abundance and happiness. While I prioritize my tasks, if I give HP level to those tasks which are aligned with my highest values that help me live my values fully, only then are those tasks qualified as HP level.

However, if I prioritize a task when it doesn't help me fulfil my highest values, then such a task is not qualified to be placed at the HP level. This is because all those tasks, which don't help me fulfill my highest values, do not serve me in the long run. It is because of this that many times people do a lot of work and yet, at the end of the day they feel they have not achieved anything.

2. **It has to be scheduled immediately** – If a task is aligned with my highest values but I have not yet scheduled it in my calendar, then I cannot assign it the HP level. How can something be my high priority, when I am unable to give it a time slot? For example, if I say writing a book is an HP task for me but I don't know when I will do it, then I cannot call it an HP level task; period. On the other hand, if I mean to do a task clearly knowing that it is definitely a HP level task for me then I must schedule it, right now. Once the task is scheduled in your calendar, only then is it finally qualified to be called a high priority level task.

Again, most people are not used to scheduling a task in a calendar. But if you want be extraordinary, then you must do what extraordinary people do. All leaders have a schedule of all their HP level tasks. The difference is that most leaders have a personal secretary who keeps and maintains their schedule. In your case, if you don't have a secretary I suggest you get a smart phone. A mobile is a great replacement for a secretary in some ways.

I suggest that you schedule all your tasks in your computer and then sync it with your mobile. Once you have all your tasks scheduled in your mobile, it will remind you with an alarm before every task is due, just the way a secretary would. You have the option to either snooze or re-schedule the task if necessary. Do not use anything other than your mobile to schedule, as it is the only thing you carry everywhere with you and it has all calendar features which are necessary for such planning and scheduling.

If you are unaware of how to use your mobile calendar for scheduling, get some help from some of your friends who are familiar with the technology.

Secondary Priority Level – SP level tasks also have two criteria to meet before they are qualified to be called SP level tasks:

1. **They have to be aligned with your highest values** – The first criterion is again the same as it was for HP tasks. The task must be aligned with your highest values, because otherwise there is no point giving it even a secondary priority level.

2. **Schedule the task in a few days** – Even though the task is aligned with your highest values, for some reason you may be unable to schedule the task right away. But you are definite to schedule it in a few days, because only then does this remain in your list of SP level tasks. This is what you call your to-do list. For example, if I want to attend a new leadership workshop which is aligned with my values of being a leadership trainer, but I am not sure of the dates on which that workshop will happen. Hence I have kept it on my SP level list, which I will schedule in a few days once I get information about the date and venue of the workshop. But if this or any task remains in my list for more than ten days unconsciously and I am not scheduling it for some or the other excuse, then you must shift this task to the LP level list. Because if you are not able to access

your internal power resources to even remember to schedule this task, then chances are that it is in your low values. In this case, simply shift the task at the LP level.

3. **Lowest Priority Level** – are tasks that are neither aligned with one's highest values nor is one willing to schedule it in the near future. These are tasks, which keep coming to one's mind but one knows that one doesn't want to do them at the moment. Believe me, there are many such tasks in our lives.

   You must have a list of these tasks written as your LP level list. Else your mind keeps reminding you that these tasks are yet to be executed and this causes stress. But when your mind knows that the task has been listed somewhere and that too under the LP level, then your mind is free of these tasks. A lot of your mental energy is saved this way, which can then be utilized for HP and LP level tasks.

If you want to be a master at time management, then you must master prioritization of your tasks. For that, you must start seeing all your tasks in the three priority levels and execute them only as per the hierarchy.

A person's life can change completely when he is clear about his priorities. He feels self-assured, confident, knows that there are only the top priorities to focus on, which will make all the difference in his life.

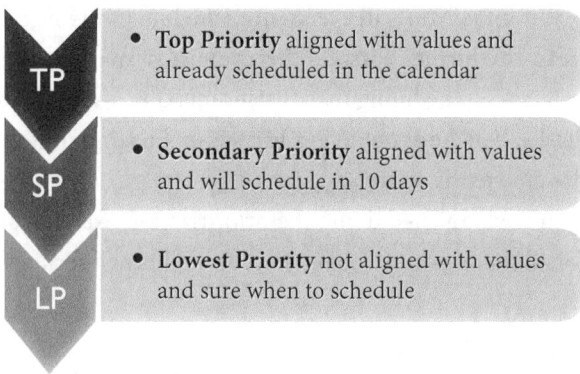

- **Top Priority** aligned with values and already scheduled in the calendar
- **Secondary Priority** aligned with values and will schedule in 10 days
- **Lowest Priority** not aligned with values and sure when to schedule

Prioritization makes life simpler and less stressful

Any person, who spends his time working on the highest priorities of life, does not have to worry about the lowest priority tasks. When you do this exercise, you will be surprised to realize that the number of your HP tasks is actually much smaller than what you would have predicted them to be. In fact you may realize that you have the maximum number of tasks at the lowest priority level.

Senior managers who were stressed out with the 'more work-less time syndrome', after doing my workshop said that now they always have time for what was truly valuable for them, by using the Super Productivity System. Other than being extremely effective and practical, this system is very easy to use in our day-to-day life.

But don't take my word for it; practice it and find out for yourself how easy the SP System is. A few minutes earlier you made a list of all the tasks you have to do every day. Now go back to that list and start prioritizing the tasks into HP, SP and LP levels. Read each task, understand its priority level, and then mark it as HP, SP or LP accordingly.

Once you have finished marking each task by its priority level then count the total number of HP, SP, and LP tasks. I am sure the numbers will surprise you because in my experience you may find many tasks in the LP, category which you no longer need to be worried about.

Now you also know what to do with the HP and LP tasks. Take the HPs and schedule them immediately; take the SP tasks and make your to-do list which you know you will eventually schedule in the next ten days.

Don't read any further. First do this exercise of marking the priority levels for all tasks, scheduling the HPs and making a separate to-do list of the SP tasks. You are about to experience an amazing shift in yourself once you complete this exercise.

Once you have finished doing the prioritization exercise, and when you look at all that work, you experience thoughts and feelings like:

- In Control
- Do-able
- Relieved

- Peaceful
- Confident
- I can do it
- It's not too much

Similar or even better thoughts and feelings are very natural experiences for any person who uses the Super Productive System. This system makes you feel confident of your tasks before you even start executing them. But this is not all that there is to the system. There is still one more important step to cover.

3. Capture tasks immediately

Many times during the day, we receive tasks from people, from our own flashing memory, messages and emails from people or sometimes, we make commitments to people in passing. All these tasks are usually forgotten, which, later leads to chaos because we did not prioritize them. But again, how can you prioritize something which is not visible to you?

It is extremely critical that you learn to capture tasks immediately, the moment they are received. But where do you capture them? Again your mobile is a great device which can work as your organizer; as it is the one thing you will always carry with you everywhere you go.

So whenever a task comes to your attention, immediately capture the task in your SP list in your mobile, so you can prioritize and shift it in the HP or LP list later. Everyday at the end of your day, make it a practice to go through your day schedule to check what is complete and what needs to be rescheduled. At the same time, you must look at the SP list and see if you need to shift any of the tasks to the HP or LP list. This will make it easier to keep track, moreover you will sleep peacefully.

To summarize, here is how you use the Super Productivity System everyday.

Do *not* start working every morning before engaging in the following steps:

1. **Visibility on paper** – Write all the work you need to do on that day on a piece of paper and include the things you might have captured in your mobile the previous day.
2. **Prioritization according to values** – Quickly mark each task as per the three priority levels – HP, SP and LP
3. **Capturing immediately** – Now during the day's start, remember to capture every task in your mobile, as soon as you receive them.

Now you are ready to use the SP System and become a leader to achieve more things in less time. If you would like a personal coaching session with me or arrange a session for your corporate team to help them master time management then you can email me at mitesh@guidinglightindia. com

---

Chapter Summary

▶ Ordinary people achieve less in more time, whereas leaders achieve more in less time.

▶ Leaders are super productive because they master time management with a Super Productivity System.

▶ Ordinary people are poor at time management because they have no time management system.

▶ (SP System) Super Productivity System is an effective time management system which has three simple steps:

1. Visibility on paper.
2. Prioritization according to values.
3. Capturing immediately.

9

Mastering Communication – Creating the
Response You Desire

When a person has mastery over communication, magic happens in relationships and work. I sincerely think this is a topic that needs to be paid more attention to in schools and colleges, rather than only in corporate workshops.

The quality of our lives depends on the quality of our communication skills. Leaders from every arena of life have understood and mastered communication in a way that it allows them to influence hundreds, thousands and even millions of people. Leaders understand that communication is the only gateway to connect with people, to create relationships and to inspire performance. To be an effective leader, teacher, parent, friend, life partner or to play any role effectively you need to master communication.

One of my mentors and a leader I admire whole-heartedly is also one of the best communicators I have ever encountered. I owe a lot to this man, it was because of his book 'Awaken the Giant Within' that I realized who I wanted to be for the rest of my life.

Even though I have never met him, he has helped me shape my skills, my knowledge, my communication and my destiny.

He has trained and positively influenced more than three million people in the world. He has met with, coached or consulted the US President, Princess Diana, Nelson Mandela as well as CEOs of multinational organizations. He has been a coach to sports champions like Andre Agassi, and his books have been bestsellers and translated in 17 languages around the world. His educational audios on success and human behaviour transformation have sold all over the world and have inspired millions of people like me, to create extraordinary lives.

What allows leaders like Anthony Robbins to make this kind of difference in the world, is the power of their communication. In this chapter I will share with you ideas, principles and strategies of communication that can help you to become a leader and make a positive impact on the world around you. What I am about to share with you are strategies which I have personally practiced for many years, which have helped me create fulfilling relationships and extraordinary success in my professional life. In fact as a trainer the source of all my success in life has been communication.

While there have been many people who have helped me master communication skills, there is one particular organization which had a great influence on how I communicate. This organization is probably the biggest open workshop organization for human behavior transformation in the world. It has made a big difference in the lives of millions of people in India and across the world.

The name of this organization is The Landmark Forum which was founded by one of the greatest leaders in the area of Human Transformation called Werner Erhard. While he is no more connected with The Landmark Forum, his work has been the source for its philosophy and approach.

At Landmark Forum I learnt the best definition of communication which is –

Communication is not what we talk, but the response that we get.

When I heard this definition for the first time, I did not understand it. In fact I was confused by it. But when I took the effort to understand it better, I realized that this is the definition, which will guide my communication all my life. I am predicting it will have a similar impact on you.

To start with here are some thought-provoking questions:

- Do you always get the response you want from people?
- Do people always understand the intention of your communication?
- When you communicate something to your team, do they always take it in the right spirit?
- When you give your opinion to your friends, do they always understand what you are saying?
- When you advise your family for their benefit, do they always understand what you are saying?

I am sure the answer to all or at least some of these questions is no. No one is 100% successful at getting the responses they want from their communication. So then how do we deal with this challenge?

One way to deal with this challenge is by blaming others for not understanding what we are saying; blaming them for not being good listeners; blaming them for not being receptive, their closed minds and so on.

The second way to deal with this challenge is to take 100% responsibility for our communication and be flexible in our communication style. For this you need to internalize the definition: 'Communication is not what you talk, but the response that you get'. In this case, instead of blaming the other person, you become flexible and change your own style of communication to get the response you want.

The essence of the definition is, that if I say "X" to you and you heard "Y", then what I communicated to you was "Y"; because that's the response I got from you. Similarly, if you give feedback to one of your team members to help them improve, but they get angry instead of understanding your feedback, then what you communicated was the anger, not what you actually said.

Traditionally we would argue with this definition of communication, because the definition that most people live with is: 'Communication is what I say and it depends on the other person how they understand it.' According to this definition, if two people are talking, both have equal responsibility for the communication that takes place.

People who accept and practice this definition can never master communication, because they think, if my team member gets angry and does not take my feedback positively, it's not my responsibility. This kind of thinking can never lead to the mastery of communication because now your communication depends on the other person's listening capacity, their moods, their perceptions, and so on.

Mastering communication requires a leader to be flexible. In NLP, (Neuro Linguistic Programming) which is one of the most scientific human transformation theories it is said that: 'There are no bad listeners only inflexible communicators'.

When I share this theory with people in my Advanced Communication Workshop for Leaders, many participants argue saying that no matter what they do, their bosses just do not understand their needs. I remind them, that their bosses are not bad listeners, but that they are inflexible communicators. If they truly want their bosses to understand their needs, then they must find a way to be flexible and communicate in a way that they get their desired response.

Just because you can't see a way to communicate right now, does not mean there is no way. There is always a way if you are willing to continue being flexible and keep finding new ways of communicating. But when people are convinced of the old definition of communication, that 'Communication is what I talk and it depends on the other person how they understand it', then their thinking is limited by this definition and they end up lacking in the flexibility and creativity to communicate differently.

Let's look at the example of a great leader who is undeniably one of the greatest masters of communication, he won the hearts of millions of people through his communication.

This is the true story of a man who decided to make a difference to his country by joining politics, but faced many obstacles because he was an African-American. As a leader, he was convinced that if he was flexible enough, he could communicate to the people of his country in a way that would help him become the leader of his country.

With continuous learning and finding new ways of communication, this man became the first African-American U.S. President. Barack Obama is one of the finest examples, who proved that if one is flexible in their way of communication, one can communicate and get the response that one wants from millions of people.

Here is an example of another leader who dreamed of being a filmmaker in the days when motion pictures did not exist in India. Many people came in his way, criticizing him and telling him his dream was an illusion which would never come true.

But he believed he would find a way to communicate to people, how motion pictures can be created. With his flexibility he not only convinced people of motion pictures, but he also became the pioneer of the movie industry in India. This was Dada Saheb Phalke,

the father of Indian Film Industry whose biography was made into a
film called 'Harishchandrachi Factory' which was also India's official
entry at the Oscars in the year 2009.

So if you wish to master communication then you must practice the definition – 'Communication is not what you talk, but the response that you get', and then be flexible to keep changing your communication style to get the response you want. This is something I practice every day and I can guarantee it isn't impossible.

Let me give you an example from the key note addresses I make at various organizations, where I mostly address a group of about 500 to 1000 people. When I present a concept, some people agree with it and some don't.

But instead of blaming people who don't understand me, I keep experimenting with new styles of communication which allow me to create agreement even in a group of 1000 people at the same time. I travel the world to different countries talking to thousands of people in different cultures and thus, I need to be more flexible when I communicate so that I can get the desired response from people from any culture. It is because of my exposure and practice in being flexible in my communication that today I have the expertise of addressing large groups and inspire them in as short a span as one hour.

You can also master communication by practicing this definition – 'Communication is not what we talk, but the response that we get' in your daily life. You must be flexible to keep changing your communication style to get the response you want. Here is a strategy that will help you to be flexible in your communication and over a period of time develop mastery.

Be flexible in all the three elements of communication

There are three elements of communication, and all of us have the infinite potential of using the best of all the three elements; and yet most human beings use them to their minimum potential. The best communicators of the world use all these three elements of communication to their maximum potential.

I believe that actors are the best communicators in the world; all they are given is just a script consisting of dialogues. But when they deliver those dialogues, they have the ability to make people laugh, make people sad and even make people angry. Good actors can make people feel anything, simply because of the way they deliver their dialogues and communicate with their audiences. That is why actors like Amitabh Bachchan, Amir Khan, Salman Khan, Shahrukh Khan, Priyanka Chopra and many others are so hugely popular. They can get the response they want from their audiences because they have mastered communication using all its three elements.

Think of a leader from any area of life, and you will realize that he would have mastered all three elements of communication. These three elements are so obvious that most people don't realize their true potential. So beware, because the moment I tell you these three elements of communication it is highly possible that your mind says "Oh that's so simple, what's the big deal about it, I already knew this". Do not get fooled by their simplicity. Here is a great story to understand the importance of these three elements.

Once God created three powerful elements that could be used to influence almost anybody in the world. But God realized that the infinite power of these elements can be misused, so they must be hidden in a place where common people can never reach them; only the most extraordinary people could access them.

God thought a lot about the best place to hide these three powerful elements and finally decided a place where common people would never find it, and yet extraordinary people would. God knew that there was only one place where common people would never go and that is, inside themselves, because they are always busy looking for power outside themselves.

And so God hid these three powerful elements of communication safely inside each human being, so that common people always got fooled. But extraordinary people always realized the power of these three elements and learned to use them effectively. These three elements of communication are:

1. Words
2. Tone and
3. Body Language

Simple and obvious isn't it? And yet I am sure you agree that using only words, tone and body language, leaders from every area of life have achieved extraordinary power and success. Whether you look at leaders 100 years ago, today or leaders 100 years from now in the future, every leader learns to master these three elements of communication to gain access to power and success. Now it's your turn to be that extraordinary leader, so you can also access the infinite power of these three elements.

In my Advanced Communication Workshop for Leaders when I ask people which element has the maximum power in communication, most people tell me it is words that have maximum power. No wonder most human beings focus on words. But as per research, here is the percentage of power that each element has in communication:

Communication = 7% words +38% Tone + 55% Body Language

Percentage-wise Contribution of the Three Elements of Communication

Now this might confuse you, because you may have thought that words are what we use the most, then how is it that tone and body language have a higher percentage?

Think of someone who says: 'I really care for you', but says it with a rude tone and a cold look on their face – would you believe that they care for you? I am pretty sure you would doubt their sincerity; but the question is why would you doubt them? It is because their tone and body language don't support their words. So here is the first lesson to master these three elements.

Be congruent in all three elements – Many people say that if you have a good intention, people will definitely understand you. While intentions do matter, I believe that people cannot see your inner intentions, they can only hear your words, tone and see your body language.

Let's take the example where you give some corrective feedback to a subordinate in your team with the best of your intentions to help him grow, but the subordinate feels bad about your feedback and gets upset with you instead of improving and learning from your feedback.

Ordinary people would say – 'The subordinate has a bad attitude' which may be true by the way. But extraordinary people will remember that communication is not what they said but the response they got. So extraordinary people would think – 'Which of the three elements – words, tone and body language, did I use incorrectly that made the subordinate respond negatively?' And: 'How can I improve my words, tone and body language to get the response I want?'

Extraordinary people learn from their own mistakes, take corrective action, plan to improve in the use of all the three elements and communicate again differently, to get a different response. If they don't get the desired response, they try again by further improving their words, tone and body language, and keep repeating this process until they get the desired response.

In this case they get the subordinate to realize his mistakes, make him see how he can improve, and even create a better relationship with him.

But this is not what ordinary people do. Ordinary people would keep repeating the message in the same manner and thus keep getting the same negative response from their subordinates.

In order to master words, tone and body language you must ask the following questions whenever you don't get the desired response from your communication –

- Which of the three elements from words, tone and body language did I use incorrectly that got me an undesired response?
- How can I improve my words, tone and body language to get the response I want?

Look for small improvements that you can make and then keep making improvements in your communication, until you get your desired response. Many times people tell me: 'I have tried everything but nothing really works, these people just don't understand'. And I remind them that there are no bad listeners only inflexible communicators. And when I ask them 'Exactly how many ways have you tried?' their answer is: 'I have tried a hundred ways of communicating and still they don't understand'. When I ask them to write down the 100 ways they have tried, they are able to write down not more than two or three ways of communication which they have been repeating.

Extraordinary people become more flexible in using their three elements of communication when they meet people who are more difficult to convince. Here is an extraordinary example.

During the 9/11 incident, Anthony Robbins was doing a seminar in Fiji for about 5,000 people. In the middle of the seminar, they got the news about the planes that had crashed into the World Trade Center. Many people from his seminar had offices in the World Trade Center and had their family, friends and colleagues working there. People reacted differently to the situation. While there were people who started crying, there were also people who were angry and furious.

In a situation like this, any ordinary seminar leader would be confused about how to deal with 5,000 people reacting so differently in an extreme situation. But as I told you earlier, Anthony Robbins is an extraordinary human being, a great leader and a master communicator. He communicated with those people in such an extraordinary way that he got them to take control of their emotions and learn from that situation to become stronger than ever before.

Anthony Robbins turned moments of fear and depression into moments of power and compassion simply by communicating with the best of his three elements – words, tone and body language. Fortunately the seminar was video recorded and Anthony Robbins was generous enough to share the video on YouTube so that we all can learn and get inspired by it. Here is the link to that video on YouTube http://www.youtube.com/watch?v=DRLrWUIM_g4

The question is, how did Anthony Robbins influence thousands of people to take control of their emotions and learn from the situation? While there are a variety of communication skills that he used, which I have learnt and even teach in my advanced communication workshops, there is one thing he definitely did, he continued to be flexible in his communication and kept improving on his words, tone and body language until he got the desired response from his audience.

So you see, you can communicate anything to anyone, if you master all the three elements of communication by asking these two questions and constantly improving your style of communication until you get the desired response.

- Which of the three elements from words, tone and body language did I use incorrectly that got me an undesired response?
- How can I improve my words, tone and body language to get the response I want?

No matter who you are and where you are, if you are reading this I am absolutely certain that you have the same potential any great leader has in this world. I am 100% sure that you have a great leader and a great communicator inside you. I want you to trust yourself as I trust in you, and I am sure you will soon be a master at communication and will be able to get the desired response from anyone you want.

Let's explore an example from your own life – think and remember a time from your past when you communicated with someone who was a very difficult person and yet you got the desired response from him or her. It might have taken you a lot of time but finally you did succeed in your communication and got the desired response from him or her.

Do you remember that situation? It might have been a situation when you convinced your boss about something, or a situation when you convinced your parents for your love marriage? Or a time when you convinced your friend about how much you care. Or you convinced someone to change their bad habits; or you convinced a child to behave properly.

In fact you know what? I am 100% sure that you have not just one but many such examples for when you have succeeded in your communication and got the desired response. What does this prove to you? To me it proves that you have already used these three elements effectively by improving them, by being flexible and thus it proves to me that you already have a great leader and great communicator inside you. All you need to do is nurture that leader within you and help it grow stronger by practicing it consciously everyday of your life.

So here is an exercise which you can consciously practice to become more effective in your communication, so that you almost every time get the desired response you want from people and thus create extraordinary relationships and results in your personal and professional life.

1. Write down the name of a person with whom communication is a challenge for you.
2. Think and write down what you are doing incorrectly in your words, tone and body language which is giving you an undesired response.

3. Now think and write what improvements you can make in your words, tone and body language which can help you to get a desired response from that person.

Do this exercise with a friend so that it would help you to think aloud and reflect. You can do this exercise every time you face a challenge in communication with anyone and you will find yourself becoming a master in communication very soon. Just believe that you can get a desired response from any person if you improve your communication by continuously improving all the three elements. And remember to believe in the most important definition of communication: ***Communication is not what you talk, but the response that you get.***

Chapter Summary

▶ The quality of our life depends on the quality of our communication skills.

▶ Communication is not what we talk, but the response that we get.

▶ There are no bad listeners, only inflexible communicators.

▶ Be flexible in all three elements of communication: words, tone and body language.

▶ Use the following questions to improve yourself after every instance of communication:

  1. Which of the three elements from words, tone and body language did I use incorrectly that gave me an undesired response?

  2. How can I improve my words, tone and body language to get the response I want?

10

Building Trust

All leaders are known for their magical ability to create trust with the masses. In fact the level of your leadership is determined by the number of people who trust you. The larger the number of people that trust you, the greater the level of your leadership! The CEO of an organization is one who has the ability to create trust with the maximum, people in the organization, and it is this that leads him to the position of a CEO.

Throughout the book one question recurs: what is the secret behind a leader's ability? In this chapter we will look at how a leader is able to create trust with the masses. Let's look at the following questions:

- Why is it that most people struggle to create trust in a small group of people, while leaders create trust with hundreds and thousands of people?
- Why is it that some people find it difficult to create trust in their own culture, while leaders seem to create trust in any culture internationally?
- Why is it that with some people, it takes a lot of time to build trust and yet leaders know how to create trust in a very short time, with almost anyone?

As far as I am concerned, this is not a secret but merely a blind spot for most people. We all have a blind spot because of which we are unable to see what it takes to build trust with people. Leaders avoid this blind spot, and are able to clearly see how to create trust with almost anyone.

What is a blind spot?—When you drive a car, you need to look to your left, your right or the rear view mirror, just before you steer your car in any direction so that you don't have an accident. Now if your left side mirror is not adjusted correctly, it can have a blind spot, due to which even though there is a car coming from your left, you may not be able to see it and thereby crash into it.

Now you may get out of the car and argue that the other car you bumped into came from no-where. But the fact is, that your left mirror had a blind spot and so did not show you the on-coming vehicle. To avoid these accidents, all you need is a mirror that will eliminate your blind spots and show you a clear view around your car.

An additional mirror like this can help you eliminate your blind spots and so help you see what ordinary mirrors cannot show.

People around us are always giving us signals and trying to tell us how we can create trust with them. But we have many blind spots, because of which we are not able to discern those signs.

When we have accidents or conflicts with people we argue saying: 'How was I supposed to know what you were expecting?' But the fact is that you have a blind spot that does not show you what people want and so you have accidents, which breaks the trust in your relationships. Just like cars, even we need a blind-spot-eliminating-mirror which will help us to clearly see what people need. I call this the Blind Spot Eliminating Perspective. This is the perspective that leaders possess. In this chapter you will learn about this perspective, thereby deepening your understanding of how to create trust with people. Let's use a simple metaphor to explain this, called TBA or Trust Bank Account.

The Blind Spot Eliminating Perspective: Trust Bank Account

Just like we all have bank accounts where we keep our money, we also have a Trust Bank Account with each other, where we keep our trust. With every relationship you have a TBA; you have a TBA with you family members, friends, colleagues, boss; you also have a TBA with your country, In fact right now you also have a TBA with me! If you know someone and have a relationship with them, you definitely have a TBA with them.

The following questions will help you understand the importance of TBA in relationships:

Surely you know of people, who create havoc even if you make a small mistake? You would also be acquainted with people who easily forgive the biggest of errors. What would you say is the basic difference between such people, and why would there be such different reactions to the same person?

The difference is the trust in your relationship with both of them. With one person you have a low balance in your Trust Bank Account, and so they make a big noise even when you make a small mistake. With the other person, you have a high balance in your TBA and so they support and forgive you even when you make a big mistake.

How people treat you and how you treat them, depends a lot on your level of trust with them. And like any other bank account even in the TBA you can make deposits and withdrawals of trust. In normal banks there are two basic ways of making deposits and withdrawals of money i.e. cash and cheque. Similarly in the Trust Bank Account as well, you have two basic ways of making deposits and withdrawals of trust i.e. Communication and Commitments.

- *Cash = Communication*
- *Cheque = Commitments*

The reasons I believe Cash = Communication, is because if I talk to you rudely, the impact will be an immediate withdrawal of trust in our TBA.

Cheque = Commitments because a commitment is given for a future date and will have an impact only in the future, just like a cheque. Let's focus on the cash first, which is communication. Building trust requires a lot of patience. Just as it takes time to save money in a bank account, similarly it takes consistent positive communication to make deposits in the TBA. With every communication you make, you will see an instant difference in the size of your TBA. Even though you deposit one rupee, does a bank account show the deposit in your account? Yes it does. Similarly, even a single instance of communication makes a difference in the TBA of your relationships.

In the way you communicate to people, you can instantly make deposits or withdrawals of your TBA. For example when you talk to your customers with respect, you instantly make a deposit of trust with them, which then shows up when customers want to deal only with you in your team. Similarly if you talk to your customers rudely, you instantly make a withdrawal of trust, which then shows up when the customer avoids your phone calls or prefers to talk to someone else in your team.

Every single time we communicate with people, we are either making deposits or withdrawals of trust which we are mostly unaware of. This lack of awareness is the blind spot I was referring to. Most people do not communicate consciously, thereby creating large withdrawals, resulting in the lack of trust.

In my workshops, in order to make people aware of their communication, we divide people into groups and ask them to do this simple exercise of writing down some examples which display deposits vs. withdrawals of trust.

The results are an eye-opener for everyone as they get a fresh perspective on the trust issues they have and also an opportunity to resolve them and start afresh. Please take a few minutes and experience this exercise and see how you fare in this exercise.

Here is an example of this exercise:

Deposits of Trust through Communication	Withdrawals of Trust through Communication
I talk with respect	I talk rudely
I am assertive	I am aggressive
I am open about conflicts	I avoid conflicts
I listen and give people space to talk	I talk a lot and hardly listen
Non-judgemental; don't back bite	Judgemental; criticize people when they are not around.
Appreciate people genuinely	Criticize people or fake appreciation
Making people feel important; appreciate them	Boasting to show how important I am
Being happy for another person's success	Being jealous of another person's success
Being responsible i.e. I think before I talk	Being reactive i.e. I think after I talk

Showing interest in people's work	Not showing any interest in people's work
I give feedback in an inspiring way	I give feedback that hurts
I'm humble in my approach	I'm egoistic in my tone
I'm appreciative of different cultures	I expect people to work as per my culture

The list guides you to understand your style of communication and further, makes you aware of what you need to work upon in order to start creating trust with people.

A very senior executive of a multinational organization did this exercise and realized that he had two major blind spots in his communication, because of which, he was unknowingly making withdrawals of trust with his team members. His two blind spots were boasting a lot about his own success and not listening, not giving people the space to talk. In the workshop we usually have a feedback process, where I give people an opportunity to help each other become aware of their blind spots. This process helped him to understand that these communication glitches were coming in his way of building trust.

The amazing part was that all this was a complete surprise to him. He never had the slightest idea that he was unknowingly breaking trust with people. After this exercise he not only removed these blind spots, but also created new ways of communication which helped him to create deposits of trust with his team again. He chose the deposits of appreciating people for their success instead of boasting of his own and listening to people more than talking most of the time. With these simple shifts in his communication, he was able to completely transform his relationship with his team members and increase his TBA with them.

I invite you to do the same exercise and become aware of your own blind spots and then choose new ways of communication, which would help you to deposit trust instantly in all your relationships. If you are still reading this, then I am absolutely certain that you care for people and want to build trust with them. I have full faith that if you follow this simple exercise described in this chapter; you will be able to create trust with anyone you desire, instantly.

But remember that communication is not the only way of depositing and withdrawing trust. Commitment is the biggest way to deposit or withdraw trust.

Commitment is what every person looks for when trusting anyone, whether it is trusting your life partner, your boss, your friends, your colleagues, your subordinates, your family, literally anyone.

I remember this experience from when I was dealing with a vendor trainer for some of my training assignments. He had excellent training skills and had great communication skills due to which he instantly created a lot of rapport and trust with me. But as we started working together, he kept breaking small commitments which I overlooked initially. But as the frequency of this increased, I felt the trust between us lessening. I was in a dilemma, because when it came to communication he was one of the best people I had met in my life, but when it came to commitments, it was getting difficult to work with him. So I decided to confront him with assertive and constructive feedback. In our communication I realized that his intentions were not wrong, but he had gotten used to breaking commitments and was stuck in a compulsive habit. Instead of breaking away from this valuable relationship, we worked together on his destructive habit. With time he grew to be a committed person and then we rebuilt the trust in our relationship.

When we have a good relationship with people, it is natural for us to start taking them for granted and thus blindly start breaking our commitments with them. Breaking our commitments with people is our blind spot, which leads to lack of trust in our relationships.

Here are some examples of how we make deposits or withdrawals of trust through commitments:

Deposits through Commitments	Withdrawals through Commitments
I reach office on time	I reach late for meetings
I call people if I am about to be late	I usually forget to call people if I am going to be late
Reach home as promised	Usually reach home much later than promised
I always follow my schedule	I usually miss my scheduled appointments
Create results	Make excuses
Call back or email on time	Forget to call back or email on time
I am mostly proactive	I am mostly reactive
Plan my work schedule	Do things at the last minute
Show excellence at work	Show average performance at work

The Managing Director of an organization was attending my workshop. During the module of building trust, he realized that he had blind spots which were creating a lot of withdrawals of trust within his organization. He had the habit of creating stretched targets, so that even though people failed to achieve the actual target they still managed to reach a certain goal.

His philosophy was the if you aim for the stars, you would at least touch the sky. This philosophy worked, but year after year when his team was not able to meet the actual goals, they lost their trust in him.

Success is essential for people to feel good about themselves and remain motivated to grow. In the workshop the MD realized, that his blind spot of creating stretched goals was only weakening the trust between him and his core team. So he consciously chose to create realistic targets that could be met by his team, which then helped him to build stronger trust and confidence with them. In fact he then created a new mantra in his team which was: 'go beyond your goals', which worked well for the employees who not only met their goals, but were inspired to overachieve as well.

I urge you to ask yourselves how you make deposits and withdrawals of trust in your relationships, so you could also strengthen the trust in all your relationships, starting today.

Do remember to mail me how this chapter helped you build trust with people, you never know in my next book I might use your story as an example. So do mail me your success stories. Until then, all the best and keep building trust.

Chapter Summary

▶ The level of your leadership is determined by the number of people who trust you.

▶ The larger the number of people that trust you, the greater the level of your leadership.

▶ We all have a blind spot because of which we are unable to see what it takes to build trust with people.

▶ The Blind Spot Eliminating Perspective: Trust Bank Account (TBA).

▶ A Trust Bank Account has two ways of Depositing and Withdrawing Trust:

Cash = Communication
Cheque = Commitments

▶ Become aware of how you are depositing and withdrawing trust from your relationships.

▶ Strengthen the trust in all your relationships, starting today.

Building a Great Team – You Cannot Do It Alone

A leader cannot walk alone, he needs a team. A CEO needs a great team to achieve his goals; a manager needs a great team to complete his projects successfully. In fact in the corporate world if you want to be a true leader, nothing is possible without building a great team.

Besides, you actually spend more time with your team members than you do with your family. So it becomes essential, that you have a great team which is strongly bonded. People who don't have great teams, experience many conflicts. They come to office on a Monday morning and wait for Friday! In this situation there is no job satisfaction and every single day feels like a burden.

Fortunately, it's pretty simple, if not easy, to build a great team and keep them bonded, if you follow some basic principles of building a great team. While I share some great team building principles with you, I want you to know that these are tried and tested principles used by some of the greatest leaders in the world. I can say with absolute certainty that these principles will give you a clear road-map for building a great team. These are not the only principles, and yet these are some of the best. Let's start with the first one –

Create a strong rapport with each team member: Creating rapport refers to the process of creating a 'comfort zone' with someone. When you are comfortable with people and they are connected, open and willing to learn, forgive or do anything that it takes to have a good relationship with you, that is the first step to having a great team. But the moment you lose rapport with someone, i.e. when you don't have a certain level of comfort with them and they don't connect, are not open, don't learn, are not willing to take efforts to have a good relationship with you then the very base of team work is threatened. Rapport is everything in a relationship, but most people are unaware of the rapport building rules.

Following are some principles which will help you build rapport with people:

Recognising similarities with people creates instant rapport. Unconsciously all human beings are always looking for similarities with each other. Similarities equal comfort, and differences translate to discomfort. Understanding this simple rule will enable us to create great rapport with anyone. It would do us well to keep in mind some basic truths about human nature' –

- Why do people create communities in every part of the world?
  It is to remain with people who are similar to each other.
- Why do people enjoy friends from their own age group?
  It is easy to connect with people of same age group.
- Why do people like to spend time with people who have similar habits like going for parties, drinks, dinner, and so on?
  It is easy to connect with people who have similar habits and a similar mindset.

Would this imply that people who are very different cannot be comfortable with each other?

No, that's not true. If you have the ability to accept people the way they are, it's easy to get along with anyone. But everybody in the world may not be practicing acceptance when dealing with you. So the best way to create rapport with people is, to behave in exactly the same manner the opposite person behaves in order to make that instant connection. After sometime, when you have a good relationship people may accept you the way you are, but initially everyone is looking for a comfort zone to get along with you.

Anthony Robbins once said in one of his audio programmes: "learn to influence people with something that already influences them." So instead of trying to do something new, all you have to do is try something that already works, simple!

For example, if you are travelling in a train and you want to create rapport with a co-passenger, you can use this simple technique of forming a bond by finding some commonalty that links the two of you together. For instance, you can ask them which town they come from. If you come from the same town, this is an excellent point of connection. The moment you say that, you see an instant connection in their eyes and they try to talk to you more than they talk to some other passengers in the cabin, simply because they feel you have something which is common with them, that instantly creates a comfort zone between both of you.

Another example is when talking to a subordinate who is de-motivated, first create some rapport instead of directly giving him advice. If you share about how you had also failed and found it difficult to cope with the new project initially, he would instantly open up to you because now he feels comfortable talking to you. Once you have a rapport with him, you can influence him to motivate himself and see things differently. But what if you had directly started giving him advice? Would he take your advice ever so willingly? I am not so sure about that. There is a higher possibility of bonding with your team members if you have created a certain level of comfort with them first.

So check if you already have rapport with everyone in your team? If not, consciously try to create rapport with them by identifying similarities with them and then engaging them. To build a great team, you must make sure that all your team members also share a great rapport with each other. Or else you will be dealing with petty conflicts every day. So take the team on regular monthly parties (it could be on a contribution basis) where they have fun with each other, laugh with each other and create a strong comfort zone with each other. Once they have that rapport, they will automatically work effectively empathizing and helping each other.

In this monthly event, make sure every person gets a chance to address the whole team and share some of the biggest challenges of their lives; including their moments of happiness and sadness. When every member shares these moments with each other, they will find that it becomes easy for them to relate to each other. They may not find similarities in their challenges, but they will definitely find similarities in the emotions they went through during those challenges. If you want a great team, you must have members who have a strong rapport with each other, which must be created by you, being the leader of the group. Now let's look at another way of building a great team.

Understand their expectations – The root cause of all conflicts in the world is a mismatch of expectations. You therefore need to have clearly set expectations with your team. There should be clarity of expectations on both ends. But before you set your expectations with them, always understand their expectations first. Ask them what they need from you as their leader. And this is not a one-time question; this is a bi-weekly question which you must ask them regularly. Why?—Expectations change as situations change, and so it is critical to maintain clarity regarding expectations.

Only once you have understood their expectations, set your expectations with them. If you follow this practice regularly, you will face very few conflicts and see your team performing well.

Align the goals of all team members and declare their interdependence. One of the greatest abilities of extraordinary leaders is that they align the goals of all the team members, and create interdependence for success. They declare this alignment, so that every member of the team knows that if one member fails, the whole team fails.

You cannot allow one member of the team to do extraordinarily well, while others perform in an ordinary manner. To have a team of great performers, you must create interdependence within the team for their success and failure. For example, in sports even though one member may do well, the team wins only when everyone does their job well.

I shared this team building strategy with an IT organization, where a senior manager was struggling with the performance of his team. After he learnt this strategy, he went to his team and declared that every member of the team must work together for the weekly project reviews. If the project review was less than what was expected, in any given week due to even one person's performance, the whole team would fail the project review.

Many team members cribbed about his decision initially, especially the ones who were high performers. When explained that their success depended on each other and on a collective sense of responsibility, as their manager was now looking at a great team performance as opposed to disproportionate individual performances. Surprisingly from that week onwards, his entire team became a high performing team. This was because the high performers now started supporting the low performing employees. This eventually created a lot of success and a better bonding among and within the team.

Conduct regular inspiration and team bonding training activities – A lot of people tell me that team motivation and bonding are factors that are mostly weak within organizations. My response to this is that when it comes to human behaviour, nothing is long-lasting if you don't condition it. Even musical instruments go out of tune periodically; they have to be tuned regularly.

Similarly, you must be willing to regularly condition, create inspiration and renew the bonds within the team at least every three months. This quarterly training – to create motivation and bonding in your team does not require a big budget. All one needs, is to be a little creative, as there are several ways of training, keeping them inspired and strongly bonded. Some economical ways of training your team regularly:

1. You can research team building games online and conduct the training yourself.
2. Ask other team managers from different verticals to train your team and then return the favour.
3. Ask everyone to read a common book on team bonding and then ask them to share what they learnt, as a part of their quarterly trainings.
4. Call some management college professors for training. Many of them are happy to come and conduct free sessions or at very low fees.
5. Ask one of the team members to create a training module which will inspire and bond the whole team.
6. Show them a teamwork related movie or discuss stories from real life and then have a discussion on what they learnt.

If you follow each one of these strategies every quarter, you will have enough strategies to keep you going for more than a year. The next strategy is one of my favourites.

Take responsibility for the team's failures, but give them credit for their successes – I will never forget this video of Dr. Abdul Kalam in which he shared an experience from his life. Once he and his team were working on launching a rocket in space, and suddenly the computer showed an error message, that the fuel was not enough to complete the launch sequence. After taking advice from his team, Dr. Abdul Kalam decided to over-ride the computer's decision and allowed the rocket to be launched in spite of the error. The launch actually failed because of lack of fuel. But, Mr Abdul Kalam warmly shared that his boss took complete responsibility for that failure in front of the authorities and did not blame the team even once. Subsequently, there was a successful rocket launch conducted by their team and this time his boss was invited to talk about their success in front of the high authorities. His boss immediately asked Abdul Kalam to take credit for it, and talk on behalf of the team.

The moral of the story is very simple – take responsibility for the failures of your team and give them credit for the successes they create. Imagine how much respect you would command if you were to practice this simple yet humble strategy!

In short, expect your team to do exceedingly well despite their failures, and set these expectations in the team meetings.

Daily strategy stand-up meetings – For an extraordinary team, it is critical that all the members work in the same direction. But sadly most team members are only aware of their individual tasks, not their team goals. Thus, every morning before starting any other work, you must have a 15 minute daily strategy stand-up meeting.

It's called a stand-up meeting because you are not allowed to sit down during this meeting. This is to ensure that it does not exceed 15 minutes. In this meeting you must discuss not just individual goals, but team goals for the day and put them on a white board where they would be visible throughout the day.

This helps the team to always work in the same direction. Even though they have independent tasks, they are aware of how their tasks are connected to the overall team goals. A lot of my clients have used this strategy to successfully create high performing teams.

Define team culture and display printouts of it everywhere – Many leaders struggle with their teams because they don't have a well-defined team culture. We all agree that a team, a family, a country must have a culture of its own, which guides its members' behaviors. For example, in India, when a guest comes to your house, you know that you must treat them with respect and first offer them water. This does not necessarily happen in western countries. In western countries when people drive their cars, they follow traffic rules; which in India we don't necessarily follow. The difference in our behaviour hence comes from our culture.

Clarity regarding a team's culture provides clarity for the team in terms of how they must behave. In a lot of my workshops, I've had senior managers complaining about the lack of culture in their teams. My counter question to them is, are they themselves aware about what is this culture that is lacking. Unfortunately I haven't met anyone who could answer this. The reason is that, while managers complain about this lack, what they don't realize is that they have never created a culture for their team in the first place.

Spare some time and write down specifically what kind of culture you want in your team. It would be best to involve the entire team in this exercise, as we do during our workshops. If your team is involved in creating its own culture, they are likely to take complete ownership for it as well.

Once it is created, make sure you have it printed all over the team workspace, so that they are always guided by the culture, which you have consciously created together.

Create a growth plan for team members as per their individual ambitions – Every team member is motivated only if they see certainty in their growth. They want to know how their career will develop if they give their best to their job. And this is natural; all of us want to know what the returns on our efforts are going to be. Unfortunately, most managers do not create a growth plan for their team members. This is something that extraordinary leaders do.

So starting now, conduct a meeting with every member individually, and create along with them a growth chart of their career, to help them understand the skills they would need to demonstrate in order to achieve that growth plan. This strategy may sound simple, but it is the back bone of the team's motivation. The next strategy will make sure your entire team is on track with their yearly performance.

Do monthly reviews, for a great yearly review – Most managers start the performance review process at the end of the year. But leaders always perform monthly regular reviews, to make sure that each team member is on track to achieve their yearly performance targets.

It is very difficult to objectively remember all the strengths and weaknesses of a team member at the end of the year; especially if you have many team members to review. I recently met a cousin who told me that in his performance review his boss copy-pasted the same comments in the strengths as well as the weaknesses columns. He was left totally confused about his performance; he did not know what he was good at and what he needed to work on. Later he told me that all his team members faced the same situation. What does this say about the manager? What kind of a leader was he being?

This is not the first time I have heard about an incident like this. Many managers fill in a performance review form only for the sake of it. But what they don't realize is, that due to this they lose their credibility. Now the team is not confident whether the manager is skilled, experienced or sincere enough to lead them in the right direction. It wouldn't be surprising if this team becomes a low performing team in spite of being highly skilled, with a lot of potential.

So please make sure that you do monthly reviews with your team members and maintain the monthly records in the form of an excel sheet which is shared with the concerned team member. This is so that during the yearly performance review every team member is clear about how they have performed and what kind of appraisal they can expect.

These are some of the strategies, which are simple and yet practical to apply, which will give you that extraordinary team, you always wanted.

Do remember to email me the results that you managed to create applying these strategies, on your journey to become an extraordinary leader.

Chapter Summary

▶ A leader cannot walk alone; he needs a team.

▶ These are not the only principles in the world, but are some of the best ways to build a great team:

1. First create a strong rapport with each team member.

2. Understand their expectations, before you set yours with them.

3. Align the goals of all team members and declare their interdependence.

4. Conduct regular inspirational and team bonding training sessions.

5. Take responsibility for the team's failures, but give them credit for their successes.

6. Conduct daily strategy stand-up meetings.

7. Define team culture and display it everywhere.

8. Create a growth plan for all your team members as per their ambitions. Do monthly reviews for a great yearly review.

MB Reading ②
Naps/Sleeping IN ①
Family ⑫   9   10   13
Work
  • emails • Colleagues • PM
  • clients • slides • quality
Exercise   12   12
Eating out   9   15
Vacations 11
  making money 13
being good person 16
  self-growth 9

    Numbers

Volunteering 13
Chores 14
Talking w/ my family (Mom, brother, sisters) 13
Developing Friendships
Work — articles — selling • presentations • stats
      — administrative stuff • office politics
reading books
    "   papers
Shopping
To-do lists
Clothes
~~Things/objects~~
~~████~~
BoF
wtg. loss
eating healthy
Brain bldging games

1. Being a good person
3. Exercise
2. Family
4. Work ~~Making Money~~
5. ~~████~~ Wtg. loss/Eating Right
~~3. Making Money~~
6. Brain games
7. Mom, Brother, Sisters
~~████~~ Self growth

    Naps
    MB Reading
    ~~████~~
    ~~████~~
    Penny
    BoF
    Reading
    Friendship
    Volunteering
    Chores
    ~~████~~
    Politics

~~Mom, brother, sisters~~

~~████~~ ~~████~~ Brain Bldg Games ~~X~~
~~Book~~
Reading
~~Friendships~~
5 ~~████~~ Wtg. loss/Eating Healthy
~~Volunteering~~
Chores

Acknowledgements

Thanks to:

Mom and Dad who not only gave birth to me, but also instilled in me the values of being a good human being and thinking big in life. Since a very early age Mom said to me, "You are my diamond, you are special, you are meant to achieve extraordinary success." She dreamt of watching me on television and doing great work. I thank her for giving me those dreams and beliefs, which has led to my on-going success and this book after so many years.

Thanks to:

My my mentors, The Landmark Forum, Anthony Robbins, Robin Sharma, John Demartini, Jack Canfield, Raj mali, Sahil Surthy (Gyandev) and my best mentor Indu, my wifewho gave me the wisdom to learn and grow.

My friend P.S. Rathore who helped me learn Fire-walk which gave me a bug boost in my training career.

Everything I share in this book I have learnt from my mentors and thus I dedicate this book to them. Though personally I have not met some of these mentors, still they are an abundant source of great guidance for me even today. Whenever I feel lost, I still access their books, audios, videos, talk to them, meet them and I always find the guidance to get me back on track.

Thanks to:

My publishers, Jaico Publishing House for believing in me and my mission, to help organizations transform their employees to lead like entrepreneurs.

Most importantly Indu, for being my wife, life partner, business partner and being my co-author. All along the way your valuable feedback and influence on this work and my life is profound, I love you Indu, Thank you!

Finally I would like to thank 'you' my readers for selecting this book.